Living in Longhand
Dan Holloway

© Dan Holloway 2023, all rights reserved

Published by Rogue Interrobang Press

An imprint of Rogue Interrobang Limited, Company number 11730049. Registered address: c/o Woodstock Accountancy 3aMarketPlace, Woodstock, Oxfordshire, OX20 1SY

Cover design by JD Smith Design Ltd

Introduction 7
Section 1 - Sustainable Life Goals 12
  Finding Your Sustainable Life Goals 20
  A Portfolio of Sustainable Life Goals 22
  The Infrastructure Type of Sustainable Life Goals 28
  Quantifying the Infrastructure 30
  My Infrastructure Goals as a Case Study 32
    Health and wellbeing 32
    Money 36
  Building on Your Infrastructure 58
  Bad Dorian 59
  Type 1 and Type 2 Fun: Not a Daft But a Really Ancient and Important Distinction 61
  Filling Your Portfolio 73
    Autonomy 73
    Impact 75
    Relationships 76
    Curiosity and Exploration 78
    Experience 81
Section 2 - Understanding why you find it hard to do things 84
  Understanding motivation 84
  Finding your orientation 86
    Past and Future 86

- The Barriers We Face 89
  - Internal or External? 89
  - Hard Barrier or Soft Barrier? 90
- Blockers 92
  - The perfect vs the practical 92
- The traits of ineffective goal pursuing 95
  - People pleasing 95
  - Lack of self-worth 101
  - A lack of infrastructure 103
  - Fomo 108
  - Distant elephants and undigested frogs 113
- Section 3 Creating Concrete Plans 128
  - The jacquard principle 128
  - Vehicles, Projects, and tasks 132
    - The Day 132
    - The Season 133
    - The generation 134
  - Vehicle-Project-Task 137
    - Vehicles 138
    - Projects 144
    - Tasks 151
  - Principles for Acting 161
    - Prioritise thorough rest 163
    - Do as much as possible in the green zone 164
    - "Today I will do what others won't so tomorrow I can do what others can't" 164

Remember I am the smartest in the room 165
Remember I can learn something from everyone ... 166
Don't do stuff for free 166
Say "no" 167
Make it easy for people to give me what I need 168
Be careful with cash 168
Look after things 169
Read 169
Journal more efficiently 170
Tell stories that centre me in the fulfilment of people's dreams 171
Develop compelling products and make them the best they can possibly be 171
Use tech better 172
Extract value from BS tasks 172
Develop systems 173
Schedule things in advance 173
Do paperwork in advance 174
Take credit when it's mine 174
Be memorable 174
Use the power of compounding 175
Francis of Assissi 176
Ground myself. Compose myself. Breathe. Take up space. 176
Your principles 178

Conclusion 181

Epilogue 183
Acknowledgements 185

Introduction

12th July 2015. Early

"I've done it!" I punch the air in delight. I've finally done it. But before the thought has finished forming, it starts to fade...

As you sit basking in the sun, dripping if you so much as turn to pick up an iced beer, it's hard to imagine how cold a Summer's night in the South of England can feel. As I ease myself gingerly into the folding chair, I have to focus every ounce of concentration on not spilling my precious milky, sugary tea. Sighing as my aching glutes hit canvas, I perform what feels like an act of surgical control to lower the tea into a cut-out circle in the chair's canvas arm. Even with two pairs of gloves and my windcheater's long sleeve scrunched over my fists, I have lost almost all feeling and coordination in my hands on what - to those sleeping behind the orange lights I passed through an hour ago, now miles away and hundreds of feet below - must seem like any other balmy July night.

Sweat drips down inside clothes that stopped wicking the moisture away hours ago. I have dry kit in my backpack. I am too cold, my fingers too immobile, my mind too vague, to change out of what I am wearing and into it. Besides, there are just 12 kilometres to go. Kilometres I've run several times before in training. Though I won't be running too many of them now. No matter how good a headlamp I have, the mix of tyre tracks baked into uneven ruts, sharp flint poking through chalk, and patches of bog hidden in the shade where even in summer the sun never reaches - all of that is too much for legs that hurt deep inside the bone every time they touch the floor.

I don't let myself settle. I cradle the tea for a few moments, down it, then rise stiffly from the chair, wincing. It will be 2am too soon. I have less than 2 hours to beat the first fingers of sunrise to the finish. At 17 stone and with 4 decades of inactivity under my sizeable belt, I am not one of the whippets looking to finish the 100 kilometre Race to the Stones, which takes place along the beautiful and historic Ridgeway, before sunset. But I am determined to finish before the following sunrise.

These next 100 minutes or so mark the culmination of years of effort. Of a dream that began in the GP's surgery a few years earlier when I received the surprising news that after 40 years of neglect my body was not, despite odds and appearances, wrecked. A dream rooted in a childhood being told that because I had a brain sport was not for me. Rooted in years of bullying at school by fellow pupils and teachers alike. Of standing in a cold field having a ball kicked, batted, beaten at me. Of being squeezed into a scrum that was used as cover to kick and bite the class fat kid. Of afternoons collapsed on lonely cross country paths - rather like, and not more than a handful of miles away from, the one I am about to head out onto now - gasping for breath, frightened the next hit of oxygen wouldn't come, berated and humiliated when I eventually returned last to school for being an undiagnosed asthmatic. A dream rooted in the desire finally to send my tormentors a full, furious, and fabulous fuck you.

Every one of those memories is my fuel for the time that follows. From high up on Hackpen Ridge, I gaze at the streetlamps of Avebury below before scouring the horizon for hints of a different orange, the dreaded tinge of sunrise. But on the wrinkled edge where the earth meets the sky there is only darkness.

A different memory, the distant recollection in my muscles of steps taken in less exhausted times, moves my feet when my conscious brain has nothing left. Even on the ragged chalk, watching every foot placement through the uneven light and the uncertain depth and shadow of my headlamp, I break into a run as I come down off the Ridgeway into the farm lanes of Avebury. Weaving through the looming shapes of its ancient henge I am still outrunning the orange fingers of the dawn that for thousands of years have threaded through the corridor of these stones. The final turn spreads out the last few hundred yards in front of me. Working its magic as only the sight of a finish line can do, every pain in every sinew, muscle, and tendon vanishes into the night and my legs propel me over the finishing mat moments before the sun begins to peek from behind the hills.

"I've done it!" I punch the air in delight. I've finally done it. But before the thought has finished forming, it starts to fade...

And the inevitable replacement thoughts flood in to fill the void. Just as they always have. The thoughts I've kept at bay for months, and wiped completely from my brain for the days leading up to the race. Because "I'll deal with that later. Now I'm focused on this single thing. If I'm going to give it everything, to find out what I'm made of, what my body can really do, then there's no room for anything else."

And now those thoughts that have been banging at my head for entry have beaten down the door, demolished the walls, and each demands attention with sword drawn and a bloodcurdling yell.

But one thought rises above every other. Not a loud, violent thought like the unpaid bills, empty folders and unanswered emails. But a thought that lurks, like a spreading glue working its way through my system choking and clogging every working part, and wearing a dirty suit of emptiness that gnaws along with its question.

"What now?"

Those words have haunted me all my life. They follow me like a mocking shadow, reminding me that whatever I achieve, however fully I accomplish my goals, once a goal is ticked off the list I am back where I started. I am someone with no purpose but a whole headful of worries.

I have experienced this same emptiness and directionlessness throughout my life, whatever the nature of the goal I'd achieved. It was the same when I finished writing a book. Or when I gave a poetry performance. Or took part in an international mind sports competition. Those things had been fixed points in the calendar for weeks, months, sometimes years in advance. They had provided me with focus and purpose. They had also served a less healthy purpose, one many people find their goals providing: procrastination. It's easy to justify to yourself putting off the things you can't face right now when you can tell yourself you have something more important that needs your attention.

The internet is full of articles that show just how common this feeling is. It's one reason depression is such a pervasive and toxic part of high performance sport (or any endeavour taken to the highest level). It's also a reason why so many people in sport struggle to maintain their hunger for victory over a long career once the initial win has happened.

This is not a book about how this problem arises. That's not a great mystery. If you live for a single moment in time, then when that time arrives, you are left with nothing. Rather, my purpose is to propose an alternative way of framing your goals that will enable you to avoid this post-goal comedown, AND enable you to stop using goal events as ways to avoid the day to day and the difficult tasks in life on which our general stability and wellbeing depend.

But at the same time, the methods I will share don't require you to sacrifice ambition, or spectacular achievements - both over time and at moments in time. This is not about learning to be content with the mundane. It's about enabling you to be truly spectacular by always having something to focus your attention towards. Something that will inspire and motivate you. Something that will encompass standalone events you could never have dreamed of. Something that also means getting the most impact and least distraction from those dull things we use the interesting stuff to avoid.

This book starts with a single simple premise. What if your actual goal is not to achieve a particular thing, but to lead a particular kind of life?

Section 1 - Sustainable Life Goals

"Are we there yet?"

As children we ask the question constantly. And we are met with equally constant exasperation. As though the only correct answer is, "Stop asking that question."

And yet as adults we are suddenly told that we were asking the right question all along. It's just that we weren't being nearly annoying enough in how we asked it! Instead of saying, "Are we there yet?" we should have quantified "there" in terms of several metrics, and for each we should have asked, "What percentage of the anticipated time to 'there' has elapsed, and is that matched by an appropriate percentage of elapsed distance between 'where I started' and 'here'?"

"Are we there?", we are told as adults, is not only an OK thing to ask. It's a necessary thing if we want to live the best lives. It's reframed as goal setting and having SMART targets, and instead of being the fuel of parents' nightmares is the fuel of a multi-billion pound self-help industry. (Of which, yes, this book is a part).

We are encouraged to pursue goals that have been set, quantified, monitored, and subdivided into yardsticks, milestones, and signposts so thoroughly that "When will we be there?" has become a question we should be able to answer to several decimal places. And yet at the same time another part of the self-help industry warns us that we have had the question wrong all along. "The point," this second group would have us believe, "is the journey." Enjoy the process, life is about the journey not the destination; don't be so busy focusing on the destination that you forget the journey. These ideas will be familiar, I'm sure.

I have written this book because I believe that both of these approaches miss something of vital importance. **A journey that's not going *to* anywhere soon runs out of interesting experiences along the way.** The scenery that we are told to spend our time absorbing and appreciating soon becomes so repetitive that our appreciation yields diminishing enrichment, and we can be left wondering when we get a new view.

I will outline a framework for goal-setting that will both afford you direction and avoid ever reaching the point where you have no dream to pursue; that will ensure no matter what space your head and your body are in when you wake up, there is always something you can do to make progress on your journey. And I will outline a training method that enables you to build a life that's rich and varied, without getting sidetracked or spiralling out of control.

But if the road that leads to a fleeting reward is full only of pain, then goals will become something to fear and resent, not something to cherish and motivate us. Most goals leave us feeling deflated, even when we succeed in attaining them, because they relate to points in time. They are about moments. We are either on the way to achieving them, or they are in the past. Only for the tiniest fraction of a moment are we actually at that goal point. And while the thought of a momentary reward can drive us forward, the deflation we feel when that moment has passed soon sticks in our memory as much as the brief elation, making it harder to focus on the next goal when we know how brief the reward and how long the subsequent let-down will be.

Furthermore the whole process of setting goals becomes somewhat arbitrary and hurried. We need something to aim for in order to give our lives and our actions purpose. But if our goals are points in time, it can be hard to decide on meaningful ones. While we still have one thing to pursue, the all-encompassing nature of our pursuit can make it hard to focus on the next. And once that thing is done, the emptiness that follows is far from the best place from which to work out what comes next - when the answer is likely to be "anything so as to feel a bit of purpose."

There are of course some exceptions to this. Endeavours where the progression follows a well-tested series of markers, ensuring that - for a time at least - there is always a next goal waiting. Sport has competition cycles and well-established pathways to progress, for example. Education has its succession of examinations. Even workplaces can have a tried and tested route through promotions to positions of seniority.

But these exceptions end up making the point even more clearly. Anyone who pursues the path of athletic excellence, educational success, or even a glittering career, will have a moment when they come face to face with the inevitable. What next? It's the reason boxers come out of retirement again and again even when it goes against their every objective interest. It's the reason people wake up the first morning after retiring, or the day after dropping their children at college, and feel utterly bereft. It's the reason so many high flyers from every walk of life ultimately suffer not just burnout from their high flying but addiction and problems adjusting to life without their single point of focus.

The first point I want to make is very simple. And if you take just one thing away from this book, let it be this.

A human life is a narrative.

It's a film, a story. Not a photograph, and not a series of episodes sewn together. Failure to fully understand this lies at the heart of why so many of our ventures fail. You only have to think for a moment to see that any endeavour that relies upon something so fundamentally unhuman as a moment in time, is bound to fail for beings who are at their simplest, dynamic. As much as we are made, in Carl Sagan's immortal words, of star stuff, we are built of story.

What we need is a way of framing goals that is as narrative-based as we are. The method I am using this book to explain, I call **Sustainable Life Goals**.

The name "sustainable life goals" is based, you will no doubt have guessed, upon the United Nations' Sustainable Development Goals (SDGs). SDGs are umbrellas for 17 areas in which the UN has decided it is important for global society to pursue progress.

The principle behind Sustainable Life Goals is very similar. And so is the execution, as we will see. Sustainable Life Goals is the term I give to those areas a person identifies that will constitute what for them would be a rich and fulfilling life. They are both the activities a rich and fulfilling life would involve, and the way of pursuing those activities that such a life would involve.

To live in pursuit of your Sustainable Life Goals is to treat life as the ultimate journey. But they are not directionless. They are not journeys that lead nowhere. And they are most definitely not vague sentiments such as "prosperity" or "happiness" or even "enjoyment of one's friends." Building Sustainable Life Goals as the framework for your actions, your decisions, your approach to day to day tasks, your way of looking at the world, moving through it, and assessing progress involves being very specific. Because only being very specific in how you set these goals will enable you to live truly in pursuit of them rather than basing your day to day, even your year to year, life on guesswork and fashion.

I want to spend the first part of this book explaining exactly what I mean by Sustainable Life Goals: how to go about setting them, and how to set about using them as the basis for day to day living.

I will outline the idea that to live a fulfilling life means shifting one's focus from points in time, the traditional way of seeing goals, to expanding the "area under the curve" - having a broad range of competencies that enable you to move through time and space in different ways, able to change tack to pursue new endeavours if the opportunity arises, seeking out and succeeding in new interests, or simply finding contentment in the way you live from day to day.

To help you set the Sustainable Life Goals that work for you, that give you freedom rather than constraint; and direction without the anxiety of "accountability", I will guide you through an examination of the way you see, and travel through, the world. Because no self-improvement tool or technique is ever going to work if following it means fighting against something fundamental to who you are. That's why so many attempts to turn our lives around, or pursue a dream, end in failure. Because you might think it's somehow noble to be engaged in a daily struggle with yourself. But it's not fruitful. And in the end the effort demotivates you, makes you resent or give up on the possibility of the dream you are pursuing, and ultimately burns you out.

I have always known the kind of life I want to lead. I spent more than 4 decades pursuing it in ways that were utterly inappropriate because I'd made the mistake of following the wrong advice. Most self-improvement methods focus on what we might call tactics - the actual things you do from day to day. At best they focus on strategies - mapping things out in broad brushstrokes. But while these will often pay lip service to the different ways we experience the world, in practice they boil down to "do this, do that" while adding the occasional "but make sure you do you."

What this book offers instead is a framework for understanding how to make decisions about your actions, about the things you pursue and how you pursue them. But it will also look at motivation. Specifically, while having goals that are points in time can lead to emptiness and directionlessness in the long term, seeing results over crucial periods - in particular within a three month window I call "the season" - is a key part of ensuring that whatever journey we are on we continue progressing.

And so, within the framework of Sustainable Life Goals, we will introduce two further ideas to help you maintain that motivation and translate the ongoing journey into the steps that make it up.

The first idea I'll introduce is the vehicle. Literally using the journey metaphor, this draws on another of the key units of time for motivation and results - the generation, a period of around 10 years. Vehicles are long-term exercises that lead to qualitative change in your life of the kind that takes you significantly down the road on your journey. Each vehicle will cut across several of your Sustainable Life Goals, but will tend to prioritise one of them. To think in the standard terms of self-improvement, a vehicle might be something that gets you to a position of mastery in a skill (think 10,000 hours) that is going to help you live the life you want; or it might involve getting you from where you are into a home or lifestyle where you can imagine yourself living out your days, but which you can't see how to attain in the short term.

But 10 year vehicles aren't all that helpful for figuring what to do when you wake up in the morning. So I will set out how to use them like "folders" - with each vehicle containing several, and over time many, much shorter (season) term projects.

Projects have much more imaginable targets (add 5 pounds to my bench press, gain a basic grasp of economics, learn enough of a language to get by on holiday, find and complete a freelance writing project).The feedback will also be more immediate. And the actions will be much clearer to define on a day to day basis.

What we will end up with is an integrated, layered system of goals in which the things you need to do are clearly defined so you don't have to spend the most valuable part of each day making decisions. But even those very small steps will, because they operate within the overall system, take you on the journey you have laid out for yourself. Targets and milestones will happen along the way. But they will never leave you wondering "what now?" Because they will always be an integral part of your overall journey, and not a journey's end. You will always know what to do next, and you will do so with anticipation, motivation, excitement and - most important of all and because this system is designed not to help you lead to the life you want but to BE the life you want - enjoyment.

On the way you will achieve concrete things you never thought possible when you set out. Things that add to the richness of life as they happen. And to the depth of your memories when the time comes for you to think back on where you've been.

Finding Your Sustainable Life Goals

What do you want from life?

It's the question that starts almost every life coaching partnership. And this is no different. If you don't know what you want, you will never be able to figure out how best to achieve it.

The role of any good coach, of course, is not just to get *an* answer to this question but to dig right down and make sure that you have really answered it. Not given the answer you are programmed to give by a life of social, familial, and personal expectation.

But what also matters is what kind of answer you give. That requires a level of reflection, and also a level of honesty, with which we are often unfamiliar and may feel uncomfortable. So much of the inspiration for life we see around us focuses on things that are fleeting, like holidays in beautiful places, or a particular kind of body - and then packages those things as a lifestyle. But for Sustainable Life Goals to be what they say they are - sustainable and for life - we need to go deeper.

We need, as Toyota's famous Five Whys technique teaches people to do, to keep asking "why?" until we get to the real, underlying reason that we want something. The reason that remains constant as the things it leads us to pursue come and go. If we fail to do this, we run the risk of devoting months or years of energy to achieving something we think will make us happy for life only to attain it at last and wonder, like the runner at the finish line, "what now?"

If you look at influencers selling the dream of life lived out of a suitcase, travelling from beach to poolside to mountaintop to rainforest, and you think, "yes, that's for me," what is it that really attracts you? What's the pull? Find that and you will find something that provides a framework, an outline that you can then fill in with more temporary things like travel and adventure. But the framework must come first. The light and shade within it can come later. Because at some point, adventures on beaches will, or at least can, stop - whether from geopolitical circumstance, ill health, or simple unavailability (as Covid demonstrated). And if that's what you've been chasing you will be left rudderless when that happens. But if what you identify as your underlying goal is a particular kind of freedom or experience or the feeling that having a kind of freedom or adventure gives you, then when one set of doors closes you will not feel as though your goal has disappeared out of reach. You will more readily be able to change the details that provide your way of life with its richness.

A Portfolio of Sustainable Life Goals

To help with the process of finding your Sustainable Life Goals, let me talk you through how I arrived at mine. I hope that will help you to understand the process of reflection and questioning involved. It will also give you some ideas about the areas you might want to cover. And more important, once you know the areas you want to focus on, the level of generality or specificity appropriate to setting such a goal in that area. It will also help identify the things better left to establishing vehicles and projects within it.

There is nothing particularly revelatory about the areas in which I established Sustainable Life Goals. They cover many or most of the things that make up the texture of life for most people. The exact combination is a comment more on me than on the innately valuable nature of these areas. But some preliminary observations might be helpful.

First, I have 8 such goals. This is a number that's both manageable (too many and you become scattered) yet nuanced (too few and you end up either too general, or unable to do justice to the complexity of life).

Second, as we'll see, they are quite specific for goals that are intended to be sustainable for life. That's deliberate. Not putting an end date on your goals doesn't mean you have to be so general that you have no focus. If you are, you will find it very hard to convert them into daily actions - or to know how you are progressing.

And finally, they are ruthlessly honest. Some of them might appear blunt, or selfish, or rude. Again, that's inevitable. These are the framework for your whole life. And the purpose of the Sustainable Life Goal as a way of framing your life is that it is truly yours. It is about going behind the mask that society tells you to wear. If goals are not truly aligned to who you are and who you really want to be, they will be impossible to fulfil and exhausting to attempt.

Let me start with the list and then work back.

1. Home

A fully paid place where my spouse and I both have the space we need to do the things we want and where we both feel safe and able to relax and flourish.

2. Money

£2m invested in assets.

3. Collaboration

The right kind for me. Not socialising, but doing stuff that involves bouncing ideas around with people who "get it" and working on projects I'm not tied to but free to come and go on following the "rolling maul" principle (in rugby a rolling maul is a group of players holding the ball and carrying it as a unit up the field. Individual players drop out and new ones join, but the rolling maul itself remains intact. I have always found this a helpful way to think of the collaborative groups in which I work best).

4. Recognition

By my peers. Acknowledged by the people whose opinion matters to me without an intrusive level of wider public recognition.

5. Stimulation

Able to spend as much time as I want to working on things that are challenging, new, exploratory and pushing right at the edges of my abilities.

6. Impact

Seeing a direct connection between the things I do and the world changing in the way I want to see it change.

7. Health

Having the physical infrastructure that will enable me to do all the above independently for the longest time possible.

8. Communicating

Having the opportunity regularly to stand in front of an audience and send them away changed.

How did I get here? I started the way many lists start. By imagining what life would look like if I were doing the things I wanted to do on a long-term basis - and then breaking that down into component parts. But instead of the usual "visualise having made it" scenarios, I didn't ask "what do I have?" And I didn't ask "How did I get there?" Because "what I have" is more of a symptom than a cause of the satisfaction that results. And "How did I get there?" assumes that the journey has come to an end. Whereas the journey IS the thing for Sustainable Life Goals.

The first step in examining the "I've made it" life was to treat it like a chemical or industrial engineering process, forensically separating it into all its elements. And then asking of each, "Is this one of the fundamental elements? Or is it here as a manifestation of something else?"

Before starting your own list, having a mental checklist of "what to look for" is helpful. It ensures you don't miss anything or leave any stone unturned in your search. It can also make you realise there are things you wouldn't consciously think of but are nonetheless important. My own list might be a starting point. But it is my list, and not an exhaustive or universal one. The key point is to understand the process I followed to arrive at it so that you can use a similar process to arrive at yours.

Where an area you might expect to be on your list is missing, consider why. Did you just forget it? Is it that the need it meets is not a fundamental one (for you, although it might be fundamental for others)? Or is it that for some people it meets a fundamental need, but for you other things fill that role.

An obvious thing missing from my list would be "work" or "career." Many people will set goals around their career. But also, when you think about day to day existence in the life you want to live, what is it that fills your time? Are the elements of your career all represented on your goals list? For some people they will be. I have spent two decades of my life working as an administrator at Oxford University. For many of the academics I have known, their research is something that would play a crucial role in their perfect lives, so building a career that includes research will be a way to ensure that the need to provide the necessary means for survival (money) doesn't get in the way of their fulfilment but enables it.

But career is also something that for many people serves a deeper purpose. For some it will be to provide the money to enable them to do other things. I want to come back to that when we consider finance - because if this is the case for you, it is important to work out exactly how much you will need in order to do the things you imagine money will enable you to do, and then ensure the career path you map out is able to provide for those things. That seems obvious. But it's missing in many people's life plans. Consider this as the first lesson in the importance of having a holistic, integrated plan that doesn't just include many areas, but balances them together.

For many others, career gives them some equally important but less tangible reward. I would argue that the academics I know fall into this category. I know that I certainly do. In my case - and theirs - that something is an insatiable curiosity. I want to know how the world works. I want to explore. I want to live at the edges of what is known and go on regular forays beyond it. So you won't see "career" in my Sustainable Life Goals. But you do see "stimulation." That is, the kind of activity I want to spend my time doing matters to me. I want to do things that push me to the edge of my ability, and explore how far I can move that edge.

Something else many people value in their careers is making an impact for the better. You will see that's on my list. Impact can mean many things. We'll take a deeper dive in a moment. But whether you see a particular problem with the world and want to devote your life to fixing it (protecting seagrass meadows, curing a disease, securing global food production, providing universal access to ultra high speed internet connections, or ensuring the supply of clean water in a particular region), finding a tangible answer to a specific problem can easily fill a whole life with meaning - and if you set the problem correctly (and, sadly, because of the barriers we know from experience but also because such problems aren't ever fixed but always require ongoing effort) will unlikely lead to "what now?"

Impact can also be something much more intimate, more general, but ongoing - the desire to change people's lives for the better. This is what lies at the heart of many who go into what we think of as vocational work. Or volunteering.

The key point here is that this or that "career" is not what constitutes a life goal. There is a level of "why?" you need to explore beyond that. Once you have reached that fundamental level, you can then start to ask which types of work would enable you to live the kind of life you have outlined.

And the example of vocational work or volunteering reminds us that when you come to deciding on the detail of the vehicles that will help you on your journey, you need to consider all of your Sustainable Life Goals. If you want to change the world for the better AND spend time exploring distant lands AND learn new technology as it emerges, then choosing a vocational career with long hours is going to give you one of those things. But the long hours and low financial compensation will make the others harder. It's an important part of being honest with yourself to admit that it's OK to want a rounded life. Even if that means you can't necessarily (only) be a saint.

The Infrastructure Type of Sustainable Life Goals

That introduction gives an idea of what Sustainable Life Goals are. And of the questioning and reflective process that setting them requires. Now, let's be systematic. In the next two sections we'll go through the steps necessary for you to set your own list. That will be the framework around which we'll build everything else.

The first thing to do is distinguish between two types of Sustainable Life Goal. You'll see this if you look at my list. Goals 1, 2, and 7 (home, money, health) are different from the others. They aren't about the nature of the activities I carry out on a day to day basis. They are, rather, about the preconditions for those activities. They are, if we think about it another way, the infrastructure that enables me to do all the other things on my list.

At first, this might make them seem like "career" in the sense that they are things to which we haven't addressed enough "why"s. "Why do I want this amount of money? In order to enable me to do these things." That sounds a lot like "Why do I want to be a doctor? In order to help make people's lives better." But there is a key difference. And that difference has to do with the freedom and practicality Sustainable Life Goals afford. Making the world a better place is a fundamental motivation in someone's life. A source of satisfaction and meaning. Being a doctor is just one of the vehicles available for pursuing it. At the most basic and sustainable level the thing to have identified is that desire to make the world better. That is what you want to pursue.

Money, like being a doctor, is an instrumental good - it helps us to do the things we want to do. But unlike a particular vocation, it is a necessary condition. In order to have the freedom to explore all the ways you can make the world a better place, you need to have enough money to, for example, pay the bills while you do voluntary work. Or pay for training and qualifications. Or equipment. And you need sufficient money to be free from the day to day worry that prevents you devoting yourself to your dreams.

Money, your home life (you could break relationships out as a sub category here, maybe. I have relationships in the other set of Sustainable Life Goals. I will explain why when we get there but you may want to put them here - as Maslow does in his famous pyramid of needs), and your health are the essentials on which those other pursuits depend, and will always depend. How much money, how healthy, what your home life looks like - those will vary depending on what your other goals are, just like the type of computer you need to buy would depend on what you want to do with it. This is what I meant when I said that your Sustainable Life Goals are interrelated.

Quantifying the Infrastructure

You can come back to this section once you are clearer on exactly what your ideal life would look like day to day, but it makes sense to include it at this point.

It's a really important exercise to make yourself quantify the infrastructure you need in order to live that ideal life, for several reasons.

First, it makes you really reflect on the nature of the thing you want. "I want to travel," "I want to see the world," "I want to create virtual reality games that change people's lives by making their reactions faster." These are all perfectly good Sustainable Life Goals. But there needs to be some flesh on the bones. Thinking about what these things cost; what skills and kit you might need to pursue them; and what kind of relationships will make them easier or harder will start to make it all feel real.

Second, It sets something tangible for you to pursue. If you want to make VR games, you can start acquiring the skills you need for that. If you want to explore the world's highest peaks, you can expect to have to build up a bigger pot of resources to need more than if "exploring" means uncovering lost rights of way on your doorstep.

Third, it shows you mismatches, goals that are inconsistent with each other or with the circumstances in which you imagined them happening. This is the most important of all. And it's why we're going to start with a deep dive into money. Because once you know the cost and requirements of the things that drive your life, some other things fall into place automatically. Some careers aren't open to you. In some cases, some relationships might not be open to you. Or it may be a combination - if you want to explore but also want a job that just about lets you afford to, you can't also have a house as a stable base to return to.

Identifying these mismatches can also help you to realise, sometimes, that maybe you don't want some things as much as you thought you did. And that you want others more. If you figure out you can't have a settled home life and do adventure sports, and you are forced to weigh between the two, maybe you'll surprise yourself by the decision you make. Or maybe you'll come up with a way of living so innovative you can do both - and that solution itself becomes your meal ticket.

But without doing the reflection, these simply become pitfalls waiting to derail you later.

Dan Holloway

My Infrastructure Goals as a Case Study

Health and wellbeing

How healthy do you need to be in order to lead the life you want to live? It sounds like a strange question. The answer for many people would be, "As healthy as possible." But that's so imprecise as to lose all meaning. It's also not really what they mean. "As possible" is one of those inexact phrases, a sign of an absence of reflection and planning that fails to recognise the interconnectedness of the parts of one's life. It's possible for many people to be extremely physically fit - but only at the expense of spending time doing other things of value to them. On the other hand, it's possible to be really quite physically fit, ample for what most people want to do, with very little input[1].

The key is to work out what it means to be consistently as fit as you need to be, in the ways you need to be, for the things you really want to do. The best way to think of this is to think of the "minimum system requirements" you will see listed on a lot of computer programmes - the things a piece of software needs from a piece of hardware in order to run smoothly.

What became very clear when I started to compile my Sustainable Life Goals is that the thing that matters to me

---

[1] This is a theme we will keep coming back to. 2 really significant numbers are 20 hours and 10,000 hours. 10,000 hours, of course, is the number made famous by Malcolm Gladwell as the necessary input to get to total mastery level at an activity (it's inexact and a myth, but like most myths and inexactitudes it's a useful one). 20 hours is the length of time Josh Kaufmann found that it takes to get really quite good at most things. In between these two figures you have 9,980 hours that give you very little extra benefit and you might want to consider how to use most effectively.

most is exploring the outer limits of what my body and mind are capable of. I am an explorer. Not necessarily in the sense of travelling to uncharted places on the globe - that has a decided attraction, but it is only part of a much larger definition. I want to explore in the sense of discovering the uncharted parts of something far more mysterious still: human potential. And in particular my own potential. To use an analogy from one of the sports I use to do this, running, I want to arrive at the gates of the crematorium having left absolutely nothing out there on the course.

That kind of life has certain requirements. Most important of all - and this is something I only really realised when I hit my 40s, health requirements. If I had to identify a single moment that transformed my life, it would be when I decided, in my early 40s, I'd like to try going a long way on an indoor rowing machine. It coincided with my doctor sending me an invitation for my "40 plus check up." This came after more than 4 decades of abusing my body with lack of exercise, over-eating, a serious drink problem in my late teens and early 20s, and even dabbling in cigarettes in my late 20s.

I also had a family background that read like a health warning. My father was the oldest male in my immediate family to have a heart attack - at just 51. I was fairly sure I knew what the doctor would tell me: "Forget it. And here's a course of statins to help you eke out a bit of existence until the inevitable."

But she didn't. She gave me the all clear. I asked her if that meant I could take up extreme sport. No reason not to, she said. I asked her again if there were any limits to what that meant. I'm not sure that a GP in the quiet surroundings of a small Cotswold town could have had any idea what I meant.

And quite possibly when she told me she couldn't think of any she imagined me going for a Sunday morning jog rather than pushing the edges of ultra endurance. But it was a transformative moment.

I had "got away with" my lifestyle to that point. I was determined that from that moment on I wouldn't have to rely on luck where I had any control over my health.

My spouse and I had been unable to have children when we married. It was a source of huge sadness for many years. And one of the triggers for our discovering travel (having asked ourselves, "If we'd been able to have the life we dreamed of, with children, what would we have regretted not being able to do?"). But it also brought a realisation that we were on our own. We would have no one to look after us when we were old except ourselves. Health therefore has an extra dimension of importance for us.

In addition to that, we have both had fairly serious mental health problems at least since our teenage years. We have found (this is not advice, and is not applicable to all) that exercise plays an invaluable part in helping us deal with those when we are able. From an immediate endorphin release perspective to the way in which exercise gives us the autonomy we need to stop us feeling shut away.

And also because we are both ADHD, and that means that we think better and more clearly, and are better able to analyse and work through mental difficulties when we are ACTUALLY moving (one of the things I discovered during Covid is how much better walking meetings are for me at work because that level of activity means I can give the best part of my mind to the task in hand). But we also know that this means there can be fairly long, and unpredictably occurring, periods in which we are too unwell mentally to exercise at all. Which makes it even more important to stay as fit as possible when we are able, so we start from the best baseline possible and even a sustained period of inactivity would be recoverable.

So that was the context for determining the level of physical wellbeing necessary for the lives we both wanted to live and were going to have to live. It might feel like a lot of detail. And almost certainly a level of oversharing. But that's the level of detail you need to go into if you're going to reach an answer to the original question, "how fit do I need to be?" that is actually helpful, and actually enables you to determine what proportion of your precious time to spend pursuing it, and in what manner. We needed to be strong enough, mobile, and flexible well into old age if we were going to retain the independence we needed in order to keep our lives both meaningful and comfortable. And as I'll explain in the next set of Sustainable Life Goals, independence is hugely important to us.

All of this means that physical wellbeing is a very important Sustainable Life Goal for me. It encompasses strength (because muscle mass, core strength, and bone density are key to staying active as we age. And besides, picking up heavy things is super fun); it incorporates endurance (because the kind of adventures that give my life meaning are the kind where I can cut myself off from the world for days at a time); and it incorporates a base level of fitness and flexibility (because my ADHD means there's always something new just over the horizon that will grab my interest - and the more general ability I have in this area, the better prepared I'll be to launch into whatever it is).

Money

This is the one so many self-improvement books focus on. For many people it comes first. I don't think that's because people are inherently greedy or grasping. It's because money is so obviously the tool that can buy us other things that matter greatly to us - whether that's equipment to pursue activities we love; things we find beautiful; the security and mental bandwidth of knowing bills are covered and the roof over our head is ours; the physical security of being able to live somewhere we don't feel in danger in or outside our homes; the freedom to go where the whim takes us; or simply the time to do the things we find valuable.

This book is not primarily about how to make more money. But it IS about the importance of understanding how much money you need in order to do the things you want to do with your life. And it is very much about helping you to figure out how much time you will need to dedicate daily to building that amount, and over what kind of timespan - and more important, what kind of money-making strategies will enable you to do that as well as living out your other Sustainable Life Goals. And which won't.

Owning a home outright that serves as a base matters a huge amount to me in providing peace, and one with a lot of space for the things having a lot of hobbies means you accumulate, and close to a metropolitan centre. I know that what I want doesn't come cheap. That means I know there will be a period when making money has to come higher on my list than I would like. That's one reason I have started to devote more and more of my time to writing, teaching, talking, coaching, and consulting on the subject of creativity. Not only is it one of the essential skills for the 21st century. And something I'm fortunate enough to be good at - and, thanks to many years of teaching, something I'm good at explaining. But most of all, it's something I love. And love talking or writing about. And like exercise, making money is something you'll find easier to stick with on the days and weeks when you just feel rubbish if you fundamentally enjoy it.

I also know this means that certain ways of making money just aren't going to enable me to get what I need within the span of a lifetime. And many strategies that would be open to me if I were 20 and broke but not actually in debt simply aren't possible. Indeed, one of the reasons writing this book is so important to me is because I've read so many books that are aimed at helping you decide what to do with your life if you're just starting out. By contrast, where there's not plain silence, there's an assumption that by the time you hit my age - 51 - you either have it sorted, or you have enough funds to do anything so it becomes "what to invest your pension in" (uh, hello, this is the 1960s calling. We want our assumptions about financial stability back). Or you're "part of the past" and not worth spending time thinking about when we could be exploring the potential of people with their whole lives ahead. Or, worst of all and I have a hunch underlying everything else - there's an assumption that if you're 50 and still in debt with your life not figured out, you're beyond hope, a write-off, and it's probably your fault anyway, and a leopard can't change its spots etc. etc.

This book is, among other things, something to fill that gap. Because those assumptions are junk.

Let me start our reflections on money by introducing some key concepts that will help you to form a Sustainable Life Goal around your finances. And then help you to build vehicles and projects to form your journey and integrate your finances into your ideal life.

Assets vs Income

I won't spend too much time discussing this as it's a principle that you will see discussed a lot by people whose thinking on the subject is much more original than mine.

But the distinction between money generated by assets and money generated by income is a really important one for understanding how money fits into your Sustainable Life Goals. Once you have established how much money you need in order to live the life you want, the question becomes how to raise that money. There are, of course, lots of other things with which your money making needs to fit. But the first step to mapping out what works for you is to understand the difference between making money by income and having assets that generate money for you.

Money from income, at its most basic, is the money that comes to you in return for something. That could be an activity, like performing a task someone wants you to; or it could be a product, like an item of jewellery you have made or an article you have written. In order to keep making money from income, you need to keep handing over something that other people find valuable - whether that's your time and effort or the fruits of that time and effort.

This makes income fundamentally uncertain. There is no guarantee that because you have received money from income in the past you will continue to do so in the future.

And even if you do, you will almost certainly have to do certain things (continue to provide effort or services) in order for that to happen.

An asset is something you own. And you can (in theory) convert it into money. Some assets, such as investments, generate money without you having to give time, effort, or a "product" in return. To this extent owning assets means that the future flow of money is more secure than relying on income. An investment will continue to generate interest so long as the financial system keeps working.

It is easy to think of interest generated by assets as being similar to the "passive income" that comes from, for example, advertising revenue on YouTube, sales of digital files, or other income that doesn't rely on you doing something new. But while many influencers will sell you the idea that making passive income is a matter of putting something into the world then sitting back and enjoying money for life, the two are not the same (though generating income this way definitely has benefits, and we will look at those in more detail in the next section, when we look at scaleable income generation).

Passive income from, for example, selling ebooks might not require you to make a new product once you have written and published the book. There is no new production cost. But you do still need customers. If no one buys your book, you will get no income from it. The best way to illustrate the difference is this. Imagine you have written the definitive book about quadratic equations. You publish it and make it available as an ebook through Amazon. It retails for £2.99 and on each sale you get a royalty of £2. In its first year it is, as you can imagine, as wildly successful as such a book should be, selling

10,000 copies, which makes you an income of £20,000. Your imagination starts racing. You see yourself at awards ceremonies, and the pound signs glitter in your mind's eye. But what will really happen in year 2? It may be that sales continue as they started. That would be passive income - money for nothing. But maybe they won't. Maybe people will fall in love with topology instead. In which case you would need to write another book to ride that wave too. Or at the very least, you might need to spend time and money on advertising to keep the sales levels up. In that case, the income wouldn't be quite so passive.

But suppose someone else notices your book. A group of local authorities in charge of schools, for example. And suppose they are so taken by its clarity and comprehensiveness and its relevance to the curriculum that they sign a contract agreeing to buy a copy for each year 11 student in their schools for the next 5 years, all 10,000 a year of them. Now you really would need do nothing more to generate £20,000 a year. The contract (rather than the book) would be an asset.

These are different ways of making money, but neither is better or worse. That will be a theme as we go through this part of the book. What makes one way more or less appropriate is how it fits in your overall portfolio of Sustainable Life Goals. If there is something you want to do that you know you could make money doing, and your enjoyment from life will come largely from doing that thing, then earning an income is likely to be for you. You get all the money you need while doing the thing you love. And, possibly more to the point, you have no need to accumulate a certain amount of money up front in order to fund that thing. You can earn as you spend. What some might consider a hand to mouth existence riddled with insecurity might be perfect for you.

On the other hand, if what matters to you is having a stable base, and what you want to spend your time doing either isn't likely to generate income or needs large capital up front, or is simply something you want not to be "tainted" by having to earn from it, then it's likely that having assets will be necessary. And they will take time to accumulate. But once you have them, you can forget about earning an income because the money you need will flow automatically.

Employment to Investment - the hockey stick graph of money making

Let's zoom in a little bit closer. Because even within the "income" model of making money, not all ways of earning are equal. And that inequality applies in all kinds of ways, from the type of activity that generates the money to the likely reasonable maximum you can earn by doing it. Again, none of these is better or worse, but they are different. And which you pursue (within, of course, the choices available to you and possible for you) will depend on how much money you have decided you need, on how you want to spend your time day to day, and on how much time you want to spend building before you find yourself in a stable position.

The chart overleaf outlines different ways of earning money. By and large, as they progress from left to right, the amount you earn increases, and the autonomy you are afforded also increases. The other thing you will notice that increases (until you get to the very end) is the scale of the impact each activity creates. That is, how many people's problems you are solving by undertaking a certain activity. Other factors include how important that problem is to them, and how scarce a potential solution is. The more unique the solutions you can find, and the more urgent and important and widespread the problems you can solve, the more value you bring to those around you.

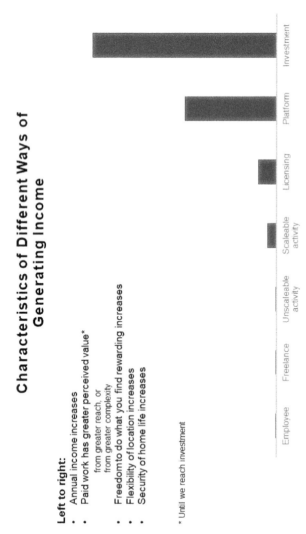

The figures I give aren't exact, but their positions relative to each other are usefully illustrative. What they intend to show is that different ways of earning money have different features, including their earning potential. As with everything in this book, the point here is to arm you with enough insight that you can make the choice for yourself as to which of these you want to pursue. And, crucially, which you should avoid because they're never going to give you what you want. That way you won't devote a lot of time and energy to something that was always destined to leave you disappointed. Or if you have to pursue a certain avenue, you can be realistic about the places it might lead

For each method, I've given a brief description of the amount you might expect to make as a maximum each year; the amount of freedom you will have in deciding when and how to work; the implication for your home life; and the kind of work or activity that might be suited to each.

At the end, it will be over to you to consider each of them, and how they weigh up against what you want from your life.

1. Being an Employee

Security.
There are several kinds of employment, with varying degrees of security, from casual to fixed term to permanent. But by and large this is the most secure way of getting an income on a regular basis, although there is an increasing sense of precarity, even in traditionally secure areas. And you will often have several protections in law that may include things like working conditions, holiday and sickness entitlements, health and safety, reasons for dismissal and notice periods.

Earning potential

Earnings are dependent on what employers will pay and market rates, and for the vast majority of jobs will be somewhere in 5 figures, for some the low six figures. This may sometimes and in some fields be increased by bonuses.

Earnings increase as...
You get promoted. Which will be for a number of reasons from gaining experience, gaining skills, or even office politics.

What you do
As an employee, you do what your employer tells you. And you will often have little freedom about HOW you do that. You will usually be using company provided software/hardware and established processes.

Who you do it for
You have a certain freedom about the jobs you apply for, but once you are in the job, you do it for your manager, and the organization.

How and where you need to live
Flexible working is increasing. And that means more time for many people can be spent away from the employer's premises (what being on site means has also changed as fewer people use offices, so if hot desking is a problem for you and you need your own space in the workplace, it may get harder to find something suitable). But how much time will vary from employer to employer and, as the time since the start of Covid has shown, may vary - with seeming long-term commitments to flexibility being rescinded on a whim. You cannot by and large rely on living away from your place of employment.

As the differential between salaries and house prices grows across the world, it is increasingly likely that without some other form of help, employees will rent rather than buy. If you are able to buy a place to live, should that be what you want, the amount of a mortgage you are able to take out in order to do so will be capped at a multiple of your earnings, placing a hard limit on the kind of home you can have.

2. Being a freelancer

Security

Working freelance can have more or less security depending on the kind of work you do. Some journalists, for example, have bylines with a publication for decades. But it is likely that as a freelancer, even if this is the case, you will have a portfolio of clients, with varying degrees of security across that portfolio. And you will not have the legal protections you would as an employee. On the other hand you will have a freedom that comes from not being an employee - your client could drop you at a moment's notice, but you can also drop them.

Earning potential

The earning potential is similar to that of being an employee, five to low six figures. Though this will likely be made up from several smaller amounts. Your outgoings will likely be higher, as you will lack the benefits that come with many employment contracts. On the other hand, some clients will be willing to pay a little more so you can cover that, as their overheads, employer taxes, and commitment will be lower.

Earnings increase as...

You undertake more skilled tasks or those requiring more experience. In some freelance roles you will be paid hourly, but you are more likely to work on a piece by piece rate than you would as an employee. And this means your earnings potential increases if you work more quickly, or on more complex tasks, or tasks fewer people have the expertise to undertake.

What you do
You will likely work on specific projects, and your contact with clients may end with a single piece of work. This keeps the work more interesting though means you are less likely to be able to settle into familiar systems - and "house style" will vary from client to client.

Who you do it for
While you are working on a project, you will be doing so to the specification of the person who gave you the work. But provided you meet a deadline, you will likely have the freedom to decide when, where, and (within limits as firms still often use their own software and systems) how to complete it. One of the tests in law as to whether you are an employee or self-employed is the amount of flexibility you have when undertaking a task.

How you need to live
You will be less likely to need to work in any one place - not least because you will likely have several clients, who may be scattered. You may, though, need to travel for some meetings with them. So you are a lot freer, and that can mean you aren't tied to high prices near a company base. On the other hand, you will find it harder to prove your continued earnings into the future sufficient that a bank will give you a mortgage. That said, the freedom of renting may appeal to someone who also likes the freedom of freelance work.

3. Selling something that doesn't scale
As opposed to freelancing, what I mean here is the kind of work where you sell your time or your service, not on an

hourly or a piece rate but more likely a day rate or a "course" rate. This would apply to tutoring, coaching or consultancy. I have called this "not scalable" because if you are working in real time you can only sell each unit of your time once. Even if you are presenting a lecture to a vast online audience, that lecture still only happens "live" once.

Security
Consultancy or coaching work will tend to be a little more secure than regular freelance work as you build up a reputation and a regular client base, and there is at present less competition from low cost high volume platforms that drive prices down. The rise of AI like ChatGPT is already changing that, though, in the educational sector. And that impact is likely to expand further very rapidly.

Earning potential
Typically you will charge a day or half day rate, a rate for a complete course, or an hourly billable rate. The highest earners who make their money this way can bring in mid to high six figure annual incomes.

Earnings increase as...
The value that you are perceived to add to a company or an individual increases. This might be making a concrete impact on working practices, directly improving efficiency, performance, or profitability; or helping an individual to achieve their personal potential.

What you do
You will carry out highly skilled work in which you have a high level of expertise for which there is a high demand, typically because it makes a high impact. Often, this kind of work will focus on **leverage points**, those parts of a process

or areas of an organization's work or an individual's habits where a small contribution can make a large difference. Typically, this might involve dramatic improvements in productivity as a result of small tweaks to machinery, production line processes or software; it might be billing mechanisms that have a dramatic effect on cashflow; it might be, rather fittingly for this section, helping someone turn an unscalable service into a scalable one - for example, by teaching them how to set up an online course or produce an audiobook.

Who you do it for
You will tend to work with (a subtle distinction, but this will often be rather than "for" as consultants and coaches are typically brought into a situation in deference to their having an expertise or set of expertises or perspectives otherwise lacking in the organization) senior figures in their field, with high net worth individuals, and/or those highly motivated to succeed.

How you need to live
At the top end of the field, you are likely to be able to afford, and have the figures to demonstrate you can afford, a mortgage on a house somewhere you'd really like to live. And because the work is flexible and selective neither the work itself nor financial limitations will place too much constraint on your home location. With rates that can reach thousands of pounds a day, you are also likely to be able to build a schedule that includes plenty of time off, although earlier on in your career seeming "down days" are likely to be spent perfecting your resources and taking care of administration, though once your resources are in place it will become a matter of keeping them up to date but not constantly

rewriting - especially if you become known for a "signature" technique.

4. Selling something that scales

If what you have to offer is something that "scales," that means you can effectively sell the same piece of effort on your behalf again and again. What you sell needn't be particularly high in value - all that matters is that once you have created a "thing" you can sell it again and again with minimal extra effort. Your income will tend to come from royalties, a proportion of the selling price of each item you sell.

The internet has brought this kind of activity within most people's reach. Now, instead of having to produce a physical object (though that's still possible - I sell decks of creative thinking cards), you can make a digital file, whether that's an ebook, an audiobook, a pdf, an image, or even a course. And you can sell access to that file, or copies of that file, without incurring any further production costs.

Security

This is essentially making money from sales. And like all sales, the security of your income is dependent upon the consistency of the demand for your product. The digital platforms through which sales often happen also add extra layers to this. Once you hit a certain number of sales, those platforms will start recommending your products more. And if you have lots of different products at that point, you can really cash in (this is why people who self-publish ebooks tend to write in series) if people like one of them. How you get to that point, though, can often feel like a mix of algorithmic alchemy, experimental advertising, and luck.

Earning potential
There is no cap on earnings that comes from your having limited time. The only limit is the size of your market. Authors who write in popular genres like romance, crime, or fantasy can make 7 figures in a year from the cumulative sales of books to voracious readers.

Earnings increase as…
Your products increase in number and in popularity.

What you do
You will spend your time making products. Because your earnings depend on the number of products you have, you will need to spend a lot of time on this initially. That amount of time may decrease once your "catalogue" has grown, because the potential value of each customer at that point is such that you need fewer new customers. But you will also spend a lot of time on marketing, because getting those customers will be down to you.

Who you do it for
Your "manager" will, in effect, be your customers. They are the ones who decide whether or not you continue to receive an income, based on the kind of product you produce. Instead of receiving instruction and feedback from a line manager (as an employee), or a project manager (as a consultant), you will receive feedback and instruction in the form of sales figures and reviews.

How you need to live
There is a lot more freedom here, because your core business activity doesn't require a particular location.

5. Licensing

Licensing involves coming up with a way of doing something or a format in which information is conveyed, which other people then use, or deliver. They receive money from their customers and pay you a license fee for the right to use your method, along with a degree of exclusivity - being the only person in an area for example. One form of this model is franchising - where people pay you for the right to a service or product, such as running a shop or a gym or a cleaning service with a well-recognised brand name. More likely, your model will involve a process or a format, such as a unique form of training. The De Bono Institute's Six Hats training for management, for example, or the Myers Briggs testing many of us will have experienced at company away days, follow this model. Trainers pay a premium to go on an accreditation course in delivering this training, and in return they get the rights to call themselves Six Hats or Myers Briggs trainers, taking advantage of the demand for the name, and having the right to use official materials in their training.

Security

As with scalable items, with which licenses have a lot in common, this will depend on the continued demand for the thing being licensed. Many license sellers try to make money from what are essentially fads. But by and large the thing at the heart of the license will have a longer shelf-life than many simple "goods" because either it takes place over time, like a course or programme, or has an obviously longer lifespan like a software programme that revolutionises a day to day task, a product *line* with long-term appeal, a new medicine, or a new process for doing something that there is no sign people will stop wanting.

Earning potential

Licensing is not just scalable, individual license sales can have a very high value because they allow the person purchasing them to make a significant living in return. The potential earnings from licensing could reach 7 or 8 figures.

Earnings increase as...
You demonstrate the value of what you provide for your users. A key difference between a license and a simple product is that you can sell a license again and again not just to different customers but to the same customer, by having the period of the license time-limited. That way you will build revenue from new customers but also continue to generate revenue from existing customers. And this is also useful for your customers - for example, you might retrain them each year as part of the license renewal, which means they always have an up to date product, and their customers know that in turn.

What you do
You will initially spend your time creating a system or programme, and a process by which you can role the practice of that system out to a large group of people. This will involve producing training materials in the case of a course, or developing and maintaining software that is fit for licensing. Once you have the product that's being licensed, your time will be spent improving it, maintaining it, providing systematic onboarding for new users, and enhancing it/developing subsequent additional products in order to maximise the value of your customers to you, as well as building your brand, so that new people want to license what you have and, in the case of training or franchises, so that customers will flock to those people who license from you/

Who you do it for

Your raison d'etre as a licenser is to provide a service to your licensees. You need to ensure you give them something so valuable that they keep coming back to you.

How you need to live
There is potentially less freedom to live anywhere you want, 365 days a year, in licensing than there is in selling scalable items. That's because some models require the licensees or franchisees to be trained in your unique way of doing things. Obviously a time comes when an early and experienced graduate of the training can do this for you, but for while and maybe forever you will be the best-placed person to deliver such training. But even then, with people paying a premium for access to your brand, you can set training courses at a time that works for you and the rest of your time is yours.

6. Providing a platform

The model employed by the likes of Amazon, eBay, and many social media companies in the digital world, "platform" is the name I am giving to anything that essentially involves taking "rent" as a way of earning money. The most traditional form of rent-taking, owning property, doesn't really fall into this category for reasons we'll look at in the next category - assets. Perhaps the most typical example, though, is the slice that a payment provider like Visa or Paypal, or a marketplace like Etsy or eBay, takes from each transaction on its platform. Matchmaking sites (that bring together providers of services and those they provide to), such as you might find in the education sector where students and tutors are introduced to each other, are among the most common examples of platforms, and those with the lowest barriers to entry for an individual.

Security
This largely depends on the longevity of the desirability of what you are offering. The latest digital platform may or may not turn out to be a secure source of rental income - but don't rely on it.

Earning potential
The potential earnings from a platform can be enormous, reaching well into 8 figures and beyond.

Earnings increase as...
The number of people your platform is available to increases. And as the value each person perceives they will gain from your platform increases.

What you do
To continue to provide value you will spend a lot of your time ensuring your platform runs smoothly and continues to offer the functionality your users want. To sum it up in two words, your time will essentially be spent on updates and maintenance. It's worth noting that the balance between these two really matters. Many social media and similar platforms spend most of their time (so it can seem to their users, anyway) on updates to add new features at the expense of maintenance that keeps the core function running smoothly. Usually this is because the original platform didn't offer a viable way of making money - platforms as a business work by taking tiny amounts of money many times over. If you don't have a way of doing that from day one (this is the advantage of marketplaces) then you will often find yourself needing to create paid add-ons (the so-called freemium model), or exploit advertising. And it's really important to realise that both of these models take you (at least, in terms

of how you make your income, which is what we are talking about here) away from the rent-taking platform model.

Who you do it for
As in the previous category, you work for the people who use your platform.

How you need to live
There is very little to tie you to any location. By and large, you will do your work online, and so you can work anywhere you have a good enough internet connection.

    7.   Investment (or inheritance)

Income comes from interest payments on assets. We've already talked about assets, and what sets them apart from revenue. Assets are anything that you can convert into cash or, more usefully, things that will generate an income for you without you ever losing the asset itself (through interest payments on savings, for example, or dividends from shares).

I said in the last section that owning property, although you receive income in the form of rent, belongs not in the platform and rent-taking category but in assets. That's because property has a value in and of itself. A platform only has value if people use it and are willing to pay for it. Of course, in some sense this is true of property as well. But its value is more stable and intrinsic and somehow fundamental than the value of a payment processing platform. And while that distinction might not be one I'd defined in an economics seminar, it's one I think is understandable and functionally useful in a self-help book.

Security

It depends on the particular asset, but by and large this is the securest of all the models we have seen. This is probably linked to the fact that many of the people who earn money this way have inherited their assets. Such assets are things that people have wanted for a long time and will continue to want.

Earning potential

The sky's the limit. One caveat. The securest form of income from assets is interest, and the securest of all tends not to be spectacularly high interest rates. This means that investments are not necessarily a way to make money quickly. The largest incomes tend to come from compounding effects, whereby small but steady returns add up to truly eye watering sums over a very long period. That period can be hundreds of years, hence the link to inheritance. It is not, therefore, usually a sound strategy to start with nothing and think about using assets as a way to make a lot of income fast. This of course matters to someone like me, starting the process of trying to pursue a financial goal in my 50s. There is not much chance for me to gain from the effects of compounding within the healthspan I have to enjoy those benefits. But there are lots of people out there with something to sell trying to convince you otherwise.

Earnings increase as...

The value of your assets increases - either because your total assets increase or the value of each asset increases.

What you do

Invest wisely and ensure your portfolio of investments has the right mix of risk and security for you. But by and large, the activity of the most successful long-term asset holders is to do nothing and let time do the work.

Who you do it for
Yourself.

How you need to live
There is little if any restriction. Even having a good internet connection might not be necessary if your assets really are secure. Indeed, not having one might stop you tinkering unnecessarily.

Building on Your Infrastructure

The previous section looked at those sustainable Life Goals that form the infrastructure of your life. They are a key part of the life you want, but they are largely instrumental. They're there to enable you to do and experience the things you truly value. In this section, I want to help you figure out what those most valuable things are.

As with every other part of this book, the more honest you are with yourself, the more useful the exercises will be. Most of the frustration with plans that don't seem to work comes from the fact that people haven't really figured out what they *really* want and what activities and strategies and motivations *really* work for them and are likely to get them those results. Not because people set out to lie to themselves (usually - we all have things we would rather not admit to, even to ourselves, and what to do about those is something I'll also look at in this section). But most of the time we simply don't ask "why?" enough times to get to the root answer.

Bad Dorian

One of the tools I use to help me achieve this level of honesty is a dedicated journal. Journaling, of course, is nothing new. And hardly revolutionary. But by and large the journals we use to organise our lives are things we carry with us everywhere we go. Which means it's possible that someone might see what's in them. Secret diaries are hardly revolutionary either. In fact they feel like one of those angsty teenage stereotypes. But at the overripe age of 51, I can vouch for the fact that a diary that's truly secret can be an immensely powerful tool.

I use a secret diary as a place where I am allowed to be absolutely brutally honest with myself. I call it Bad Dorian. After the Oscar Wilde novella The Picture of Dorian Gray. The basic plot revolves around Dorian's desire to live a hedonistic lifestyle without paying the physical price for doing so. He achieves this through a portrait of himself, which he keeps locked away. Whatever vice Dorian indulges in, no trace is left on his person. But the portrait transforms into that of an unrecognisable monster as it becomes a mirror for Dorian's soul.

I'm not suggesting that people are motivated by vices they would keep secret from the world at all costs. But for most of us, a truly honest reflection would reveal things about what makes us tick that we would rather other people didn't get to see[2]. And if we don't have a public space where we can openly talk about these things (even if it's just figuring out how important, "getting revenge on the kids who made my life hell" or "proving Mr O'Brian the Geography teacher wrong" actually is in our core motivation), then we need to create a private space.

Think of your secret journal as the equivalent of the desert or wilderness. It is the place you go at a key point in your life to confront your inner demons, discover your true self, and bring the strength and significance of that discovery back with you into your regular life, where you can use it to confront more external obstacles.

Type 1 and Type 2 Fun: Not a Daft But a Really Ancient and Important Distinction

Most of us are familiar with the terms type 1 and type 2 fun. The terms belong to something that goes by the rather sinister sounding title of "the fun scale." Originating in the world of outdoor pursuits and extreme sports, the fun scale seems to have been given that name in the mid 1980s. Type 1 fun is what most people would call, well, fun. It's the kind of thing you do that you enjoy while you're doing it. Like a merely moderately scary roller coaster, a bike ride or walk on a summer's day through stunning scenery, sex, or your favourite meal. We might look back fondly on type 1 fun in the way we do when we flip through a photo album and remember the good times.

Type 2 fun is the kind of thing that might not feel quite so enjoyable when we're actually doing it. For example if that walk, rather than through the valley floor, was up the steep valley sides and then along the precipice edge looking back down. Running an ultramarathon, wingsuit flying, learning a new skill that you find really hard. These are all type 2 fun.

But for those who preach the value of type 2 fun, the real difference comes when doing the actual thing has stopped (as someone who's run a handful of ultramarathons and hopes to run more than a handful more, I will admit to some bias here). Unlike type 1 fun that you look back on with a smile but is essentially easy come easy go, type 2 fun is something we will look back on with immense satisfaction. We will not only be glad we did it, we will be glad we are the kind of person who did it. And we will lead richer, more rounded and rewarding lives for having done it, and discovered we are that kind of person.

Outdoor sports may have given us the terminology of type 1 and type 2 fun, but the concept is something we're all familiar with. Society tends to look down on type 1 fun, dismissing it with terms like "frivolous" and "shallow" and "transient". Many of the moral panics of the 20th century (and beyond), whether around alcohol, drugs, casual sex, or rock and roll could be put down to a demonisation of type 1 fun. A lot of the time that's down to the perceived social fragmentation it causes as people seek their own personal pleasure rather than the greater good of society. That in turn means we often associate type 2 fun with censorious or fuddy duddy figures. Those pesky grown-ups, we imagine, are pretending dull, drudgerous, and plain difficult tasks like reading and debating, keeping fit, learning mechanical skills or calibrating the movement of the stars are "fun" by inventing the notion of "type 2 fun."

Actually the distinction between fleeting, usually sensual or sensory-based, fun or pleasure on the one hand and richer, more lasting and satisfying happiness or enjoyment on the other is one that's as old as philosophy, and probably as old as the first parents trying to convince their children to stop running around and eating sweet tasting stuff and buckle down to some useful work instead with the promise of a pay-off in the long term.

In the late 18th and early 19th centuries the distinction was at the heart of a ferocious debate between the British philosophers Jeremy Bentham and John Stuart Mill. Both were advocates of what we call utilitarianism. That's the moral system which proposes that the best action to perform in any situation is the one that leads to the greatest amount of happiness for the greatest number of people.

But Bentham and Mill meant very different things by "happiness." For Bentham, human nature was very simple. We are, he thought, essentially pleasure-pain machines. That is, we either find things pleasurable or painful. We should try to maximise the amount of pleasure we feel and minimise the amount of pain. That makes him what we call a hedonist. A life of type 1 fun would have been something he wholeheartedly approved of. And if he were drawing up his Sustainable Life Goals, they would have been designed around pleasure (with possibly a nod to staying a little bit healthy because being ill from eating too much and having your life cut short by excess wouldn't optimise the pleasure-pain equation).

Mill was clearly horrified. For him, reducing human nature to pleasure and pain was to take us down to the level of the animals. It was, as he put it, far better to be an unhappy Socrates than any kind of pig, even one living its best life. Human nature was something deeper, something more than just sensation. We are capable of feeling satisfaction. Of feeling curiosity, empathy, sentiment, hope - the stuff of Shakespeare not the stuff of the mosh pit.

My purpose in outlining this distinction isn't to point you in the direction of one form of pleasure or another. It's to keep you asking questions until you have considered all the possibilities and worked out exactly what it is that motivates you.

In all probability, your ideal life will be more complex than simply "I want to spend my days eating jellies" or "I want to live in the library." Though it might also be either of those things. What matters is that you understand that mix, and the infrastructure you will need in order to maximise it. Only then can you start to put actions in place that will help you on the way.

When you alight on something that gives your life value, the question to ask yourself isn't "is this something I should enjoy or not?" Rather, ask yourself the following questions:

- Is this something I enjoy for itself, or something I enjoy because it enables me to do something else? If the latter, then what is that other thing? Because that's what really motivates you.
- What other things do I need to put into place in order to be able to enjoy this thing? Because those things - whether that's a level of physical health, a level of income, or a home in a particular location - will need to be part of your infrastructure goals.
- Is this really something that's sustainable? It's great to have a list of those things you'd like to do once in a lifetime. And some of them will need a lot of very specific work - if you want to perform at the Royal Albert Hall, for example, you're going to need to start practising! But these are still "point in time" goals. They aren't Sustainable Life Goals. The underlying Sustainable Life Goals will likely be things like having the fitness levels to enter your once in a lifetime race if the opportunity arises (or to have a realistic chance of being a great team member if you see someone say they're leading an expedition to that place you always wanted to go); or having the kind of money that means whenever the chance arises to visit a place you

thought you'd never get the chance to see, you can do so whatever it costs

Asking those questions will help you to avoid thinking of something as a Sustainable Life Goal that isn't. And that will help to avoid frustration down the line when you hit a situation where you've done what's on your list and you still feel discontented.

It is absolutely still important to keep those more transitory things in mind, though, when you are setting your infrastructure goals. It's good to remind yourself that the reason you want £2 million in the bank is because that's the figure that gives you the freedom for the rest of your life to ski all the slopes you want to; or always drink the best wine. Whatever it is.

Because those infrastructure goals can be really easy to get hung up on. We can end up pursuing them single-mindedly without remembering why. And that leads us to some dark and unsatisfying places. It also means we pursue them beyond the point of their usefulness. It might well be that we discover the things we want to be able to do at the drop of a hat cost more than we first realised - or get spiked by an inflation the interest on our assets can't cover. And in that case, we need to reassess how much money we need. But the reason should remain the same. We want the money to help us to do the things. Once we have enough for that purpose, we're good. We need to make sure we keep that amount (hence the Sustainable of Sustainable Life Goals). But we can stop directing our energy at getting more. The problem is, in practice that's when it becomes hardest to just stop.

I recommend taking the following approach to your infrastructure goals.

- Be as concrete, and detailed, as you can. And base that detail on the best research you can do. How much income do you need? How do you want to get that income? (for example, £30,000 a year net income from interest on assets; £60,000 per year in royalties from scalable goods) How strong do you want to be? How flexible? How much endurance do you want to have? (In the top 30% for my age group at the bench press? Able to walk 10 miles carrying a decent sized pack without having to stop?) Where do you want to live (A 5 bedroom house with a music room and an indoor pool? A house big enough for my partner and me in Cornwall with a small flat in Paris and a Winnebago to travel in?)
- How happy are you that you have set these at the right amount? At this stage, I recommend you start putting some actual numbers to your attitude to these goals. This is going to be a key part of the approach I am advocating in this book, which is to see your life as something whole, interconnected, that cannot be boiled down to one single thing but rather has to be a balance. This is how I recommend you do it.
    - Write down each of these concrete infrastructure goals.
    - On a scale of 1-10, write down how happy you would be with your life at the point where you have hit each of those numbers.
    - Now, I want you to imagine that you overshoot each of those targets in turn. Did you set yourself a target of £2 million in assets? Imagine you have £5 million. Was your aim to be in the top 25% of your age group for your Parkrun time? Imagine you are top 10%. Did

Living in Longhand

you want a 4 bedroom house in the town you grew up in? Imagine you have a 5 bedroom house - and a flat by the coast.
- How happy would you be if you overshot all of your targets like this? What about if you only overshot one of them? Try each in turn and, again, score out of 10. If you want to give a higher score than the initial figure but you can't because you already gave a 10, then downgrade the initial figure - because you have just shown that it wasn't a 10 after all.

- Overshooting the numbers you set for yourself shouldn't improve your happiness score. If it does, you need to change those numbers and repeat the exercise until that no longer happens. This is a good exercise in itself for helping you to figure out exactly the level of infrastructure your best life depends on.
- But the really important bit is this. Every 6 months, repeat this exercise. As always, do so absolutely honestly.

What you're doing is keeping an eye out for mission creep. If you find that your original infrastructure goals no longer make you as happy as the idea of overshooting them, then something important has changed. You need to acknowledge that and do something about it.

It may be that your progress to date really has caused a recalibration. Maybe you never realised just how much you love a life of adventure until you started, and now you know that you will never be satisfied until you see every rainforest in the world, for example.

But it's also possible that you are getting carried away by the initial wave of enthusiasm for something. Which is great. But it can also lead you to downplay other parts of your overall Sustainable Life Goals. Maybe you feel that health and money need to be upped for this new adventurous life but you can forget about the 5 bedroom house you were going to spend your twilight years chilling in. That's the kind of thing you need to keep your eye on. Because if it is something fleeting but you end up neglecting a vital part of your original overall package for years as a result, you're storing up trouble.

Life changes. Life ambitions change. But by paying so much attention to getting your Sustainable Life Goals right at this point, the aim is not just to stop yourself reaching the "what now?" point when you "get there" - it's also to give you something robust enough to avoid the shorter term changes derailing the longer term plans. And if that language sounds familiar, it should - it's the same philosophy as having a portfolio of investments that will ride out short term fluctuations and see you safe in the long term.

This kind of regular check-in will also help you spot any tendency to become overly focused on any one thing. It's very easy to see early success in one area, and for the encouragement that gives you to lead you to focus on it more, and for a feedback loop to form, leading to a fixation with that one thing. This can be harmful to your other, wider ambitions, creating a loss of balance. It can also, sometimes, become harmful in itself. For me it has in the past led to the edge of eating disorders, for example. That's one reason why I keep my physical goals deliberately broad and spread across speed and endurance and strength. That stops me saying, "If I was a bit thinner I'd be better still" or "If I had just a bit more muscle..." Because while each of those might sound plausible if my goal was to be fast over long distances or be able to lift a lot of weight, it makes no sense in the context of all-around fitness.

The idea of checking in at least every six months is that you catch any tendency to fixate or drift before it becomes so ingrained that it's harder to deal with.

If you do see the numbers changing, that's the point when you need to bring yourself back to your full portfolio of Sustainable Life Goals. You need to look at them again. Really honestly. Is this still what you want? Is the infrastructure you thought would help you still the one most likely to support your intentions?

If it is, you need to recentre around those and break the slip into single-mindedness. This is one of the reasons I developed the Jacquard Training System, which we'll look at in a later section. But the principle behind it is very simple. It recognises that you can't give your all to every area you want to improve, all the time. So you do a bit of everything. But at any one time, one or two things are your focus. And what those particular areas of focus are rotates over time.

If you need to recentre yourself around your goals to avoid fixation, that means it's time to switch the main thing you're spending your time on. And if the thought - or the practice - of that makes you feel anxious because you can spend less time on the thing you had been focusing on, that's a sure sign you were heading down a path that would have taken you away from your balanced goals.

It's also really important to acknowledge that anxiety occurs when you scale back from something that has been part of your goal-pursuing behaviour. This is absolutely to be expected. And it's why it's so important that you keep sight always of the overall portfolio of Sustainable Life Goals.

It is not the case that stepping back from one activity means you are taking your goals less seriously. It means you are taking them, and your life as a whole, more seriously. Because you are taking active measures to ensure that you devote yourself to progress in its fullest sense. To carry on pursuing a single thread of your goals relentlessly would actually mean relegating your Sustainable Life Goals in your priorities.

This is the point at which to mention the controversial M-word. "Mindfulness" has become such a buzzword that it is to all intents and purposes meaningless to talk about it in many contexts. Part of the problem, and one of the reasons it provokes such strong reactions, is that it has been misrepresented and, not to put too fine a point on it, made to fit whatever programme or app someone happens to be selling at any given time.

I am very lucky, living in Oxford, to have studied mindfulness at Mark Williams' research centre. Mark learned directly from John Kabat-Zinn who brought mindfulness to the world in its current form. When I learned it there was none of the hype or faux-spirituality or tech-bro speak that has accreted to it in recent years.

So I still think of what I am describing here as a mindful approach. Because that's what it is, in this classical sense of taking regular time to stop, move my attention from the world around me and pay close attention to what is happening in my mind and body at that moment, recognising and acknowledging what I find, assessing what that means, making a choice about how to proceed from the exact state I find myself to be in, and then proceeding to act out that choice as I move my awareness out of my inner landscape and back to my journey through the world.

Another word for this kind of deliberate reflection is intentionality. It's a word I like because it's very active. And it emphasises that progress comes, and in this context is maintained, when we continually bring ourselves back to what it is we are hoping to achieve. When we ensure we are continuing to take actions on a daily basis that will get us to where we are going in life. And when we regularly look up from the detail and assess whether that detail is still directed towards the larger picture.

The other key point about this cycle of reflection and intention is that it reminds us of the extent of our decisions. Specifically, it does not let us drift along in patterns of behaviour that no longer are - or never were - useful. It doesn't allow us to carry on in default behaviours and to convince ourselves that the usual way of doing things is something that just somehow "happens." When we are intentional, we are constantly reminded that inaction is a choice as much as action. That pursuing any course is a choice in which we have played a part - even if that course is the one we have always taken.

Finally, the pursuit of a single strand of our goals can tip, if we are not intentional in this way, and if we don't regularly make ourselves switch the emphasis in our training, into anxiety and fixation that becomes disordered. This happens most commonly with weight and exercise. Establishing regular eating habits as part of maintaining a level of health we need for the life we want to live can become something we fixate on very easily. I've been there on many occasions, sitting at my desk running numbers for hours on end while my head is light and my stomach cramps and I picture the immediate relief that a meal would bring before I have visions of horror at the shape I would take on if I actually went ahead and had that meal.

The result was that I would end up too low on energy to actually train. And too low on bandwidth to do anything else to a satisfactory level. Including fighting for my own health. Being regular about and honest in your assessments, in the way I suggest here, gives you more chance of spotting early warning signs. Being intentional about what you do with that information can point you back to the steps that will help your overall goals and stop you getting derailed.

Filling Your Portfolio

Everyone's Sustainable Life Goals will vary. And the purpose of this section of the book is to give you the technique for finding yours. Not telling you what they should be. In order to make sure you carry on the process of asking questions until you have found the best answers, these are areas you should consider looking at before deciding your portfolio is full.

Autonomy

Autonomy is the umbrella term given to the extent of the freedom we have, or lack, when it comes to deciding what we do with our lives - in the longest term sense of working through a book like this and assessing how many options we have in our life; and in the day to day sense of deciding what shoes we will wear and what we will have for lunch - and where, and when, and with whom. It is something most people value immensely but usually forget to list when they think about what they value. Which is why I've placed it at the top of the list here. It's something I talked about a lot when I went through different ways of bringing in an income. Some forms of earning allow you more freedom over how you work and where you work, what you work on, and who you work for.

Autonomy is something that many of us might not realise matters to us. And for that reason, it's important to understand the language and feelings we might use that demonstrate a frustration with a lack of autonomy in our lives. We may use phrases like "There's no way out," "I feel trapped in this situation/job," or "I'm sick of only ever doing what my manager tells me in the way they tell me and having no control over how I get things done." This sense of being trapped can apply to many parts of our lives.

For many people, work is the place where we feel a lack of autonomy. The author Daniel Pink, in his celebrated writing on how to motivate people in the workplace, lists the three keys to a satisfying employee experience as "autonomy, mastery, and purpose." We have already looked in this book at how we can tailor the way we generate the income we need to ensure we also have the level of autonomy we need to make that as satisfying as possible.

Home and relationships are also places we can really feel a lack of autonomy. I am not, as I have said before, writing this book to give relationship advice (though if I were, I would highlight the importance of everyone within a relationship both having the freedom to set their own boundaries and having autonomy within those boundaries), What matters here is that you are aware of the areas in which autonomy matters to you, and what autonomy means in those spaces.

It's also, again, important to consider the whole picture of one's life. We can often tolerate a lack of control in one area of our lives if we have an outlet in another. It's as if the need for autonomy is like the build up of steam under a pie crust. It doesn't matter so much where in the crust we release the steam in order to stop the pastry exploding and covering the oven with gravy. It just matters that we do. In relationships, for example, partners can often be very happy going along with things they may not necessarily find interesting or particularly rewarding but make their partner pleased, if they are able to keep time and space for the things that matter to them - whether that's room for a collection only they cherish, or time to pursue a hobby that interests only them.

Impact

Many people would say they want to change the world. Or even to save it. Some would talk about making people's lives better. Or leaving a legacy, actions or things by which or for which they will be remembered.

People who tackle many of the world's biggest problems - or even what might feel like really small ones - all to some degree have this one thing in common. They want to have an impact. They want to make a difference. They want to know that they leave the world changed from how they found it. Not in the trivial sense that every action we ever take changes something in some way. Wanting to create impact is about change that is somehow significant and somehow meaningful.

Both of those terms, significant and meaningful, are of course subjective. What it means to change the world in these ways will depend first and foremost on what you value.

Those things we value tend to be things close to us in space (related to our day to day lives - such as problems we have encountered, illnesses we or those we love have experienced, and so on) and close to us in time (we can see an obvious connection between something we can do and a tangible result).

The other vital component for something to crystallise as a value that motivates us in life, is the belief that we can do something to contribute towards it. If solving a problem that has particular meaning to us is going to become a Sustainable

Life Goal, then to avoid frustration we need to believe at some level that we can contribute something significant and meaningful to the solution. That might be tackling one element of the problem itself. It might be bringing together a team that can solve it. Or it might be, as effective altruists have become known or notorious for advocating, earning enough money to fund other people who can do those things.

This is another of those areas that requires detailed and honest reflection. And because we are talking about Sustainable Life Goals, and not just what you want for your birthday, this again means digging beneath the things society tells you to value. You have to find the thing that matters to you. The problem that touches your life in a way nothing else does.

If you can't find anything, that's also fine. And important to admit. Leave a placeholder here. Because one day you might find something. And in the meanwhile move on.

Relationships

"Relationships" covers every part of the human connections that shape our lives, from our families and friends to our partners and colleagues. There are very few if any interactions we carry out on a daily basis that do not in some way involve relationships. So understanding what we want from and what we bring to relationships is something that affects us on a daily basis. Not understanding the things that frustrate us so that we can take time to work on changing them, can leave our lives miserable. Not understanding what gives our life purpose and pleasure in relationships can leave our lives lacking a richness they could otherwise have.

As with every other area in your Sustainable Life Goals, when it comes to relationships it's essential that you are honest with yourself. Unfortunately, as with money, this can be an area where we find it really hard to be honest. In part because we are brought up with so many codes and taboos around relationships that encourage us to believe some wishes are inherently bad or unworthy. And in part because from our earliest days, it can be relationships that don't work, with our parents for example, that shape our lives in ways that make us deeply unhappy, and we spend our whole lives thereafter finding ways to protect ourselves from having to confront the issues that result.

It is not the role of this book to offer the kind of advice that would best come from a relationship counsellor or a therapist. But I do want to offer you some ways you might find helpful for putting a tangible value on what it is you value in relationships that you can then use when drawing up and assessing your progress towards your Sustainable Life Goals.

You could think in terms of the different people with whom you have relationships: friends, lovers, family, colleagues, those who manage you, those you manage, those you meet casually day to day.

But I have found it more helpful, in analysing each of these, to think in terms of the qualities that make each of these relationships feel "right." And the things I notice by their absence. Breaking it down in this way, relationships almost fall into a category within life that needs a further kind of "why?" That is, I value different relationships for what they contribute to my life - and it is those things that ultimately matter to me. Relationships are more vehicles that enable me to enjoy those things, and not the goals in themselves.

This may feel like a very cold and mechanical way to talk about something so fundamentally human as relationships. But when it comes to establishing a pattern for one's whole life, that is the kind of honesty and refusal to accept convention that's vital in order to avoid frustration and resentment and dissatisfaction. It can also be very helpful in evaluating particular relationships so that one never gets caught in a cycle of continuing with something just because "that's the way things are."

So what are those qualities relationships offer? I would count, and urge you to reflect on, belonging, purpose, shared experience, discovery and adventure, pleasure, fulfilment, and one thing we have already looked at: impact.

Some relationships will be part of the most fundamental fabric of the value in your life. A life partner; a child; someone you meet once on a through hike, fall into an effortless and deep conversation with, unlock secrets about yourself in the company of and share sights, fears, dangers and triumphs with and then never see again - each of these can give shape to your life in the most wonderful way.

Relationships can also open doors to places you might not otherwise go - to adventure or creating impact in the world, inventing something new, complementing each others' skill sets, pushing each other to challenges.

Curiosity and Exploration

Living in Longhand

Curiosity is fundamental to human motivation. Many of us know almost intuitively - and see the idea reinforced every day in popular culture tropes such as Homer Simpson staring at a big red button - that if we really want to get someone to do something, the best way is to tell them it's forbidden.

Whether it's an ocean horizon we can't see beyond, a shelf that's just out of reach, a locked door, a sealed box, or a line on the map marking off the words, "here be dragons" - curiosity propels us to take risks we otherwise wouldn't take; to dream of having a different life from our parents and our peers. It is the driving force behind art and industry alike. It impels us to love and compassion for the unfamiliar. And it impels us to greed, covetousness, and violence to obtain that which is not yet ours. It drove Adam and Eve out of the Garden of Eden. And it drove every attempt to return us to it.

And on the subject of apples, curiosity may be many things to many people, but the one thing we can't do, in the words of Steve Jobs, is to ignore it.

To help you discover the role curiosity plays in your Sustainable Life Goals, I want to discuss two facets of curiosity.

First, the main barrier to curiosity as a motivation for people to act, or dream, or set out to tackle the things that matter to them most, is a lack of resources. Those resources could be financial freedom, physical prowess, technical skills, autonomy to explore one's own world without permission, or simply mental bandwidth. But understanding the factors that currently limit your curiosity and its ability to shape your life is fundamental to understanding how to give it the fullest role in your life. Or even the role you would love it to have, if only you had the space to figure that out.

Curiosity, more than any other thing on this list, relies on getting your infrastructural Sustainable Life Goals sorted out. So this is something that may need an iterative approach. Which is another reason why revisiting this portfolio of Sustainable Life Goals every 6 months is important. As you free up more bandwidth with improving finances you may find your curiosity grows. You should certainly expect to see it grow. Indeed, if you start out at this point saying, "I haven't got the time or space to think about anything more than getting my life straight," that's fine, but put a bookmark in to make sure you revisit your curiosity the next time around, just to see if there is a correlation in growth.

I would also encourage you to make this an area where you really go to town with brutal honesty. Try to remember back to times in your childhood, if you can do so safely, when you allowed yourself to dream. Maybe there weren't any. But maybe there were, and the memory is in there somewhere. Is it the case that if, even if it seems impossible right now, you were to find yourself without the money or relationship or career or other worries that are eating your bandwidth right now, you know that you would in some way value curiosity in whatever form it takes? That might be learning in a library, exploring the internet, or getting out of the front door and seeing where it leads you.

I absolutely understand that so long as your circumstances may not permit you to spend time pursuing this rediscovered curiosity it isn't be helpful to pin a reminder to your fridge door. For many people, myself included, reminders of things you actually can't do right now but desperately want to can be more harmful than inspiring (though for others the opposite is true. In which case take this revelation about yourself, stick it to your fridge, make it your desktop screensaver, put it on the inside of your front door so you see it every morning before you leave - go at it). If that's the case, the key step you can take is to go back to your infrastructural goals and work at the tiny steps on those that will slowly release bandwidth. And if you manage to do that, see if, over time, your ability to face and be motivated by your curiosity returns. It may provide sufficient structure and motivation to help you if you simply know that you want to be curious.

The second part of curiosity is how it relates to our relationships. Many of us want to experience new things not just because those experiences satisfy something within us, but because we want then to share the story with others. Curiosity can provide social currency. And social capital - to have done something our friends or peers have not provides us with status, as well as acting as a conversational glue. Many of us want not only to explore new places, but to come back from those places, tell our friends - and then take those friends back on a return journey for which we act as their guide.

Understanding which elements of curiosity matter to you will help you to find ways to ensure that your life is filled with ways to continue to meet that need. In my experience, curious people are very good goal setters, in part because curiosity leads to dissatisfaction with the status quo in a positive sense. If you are reading this book at all, I would expect you to be naturally driven by curiosity. "Who could I be?" is, after all, the most curious question we can ask. We'll talk about this a little more when I talk about "directedness in time" in a later section. Curious people tend to live in the future rather than the past, always wondering what might be out there waiting to be discovered rather than looking back on what has gone before, waiting to be remembered.

Experience

Finally, consider experience as a thing in itself. And by experience I mean what it is actually like when you are doing a particular thing. The sensual, intellectual, in the moment feeling you have as you partake in an activity. This is similar to the discussion of type 1 and type 2 fun to the extent that discussion looked at whether we like to enjoy things more in the moment or more when we look back on the moment. But it is more detailed. It asks what it is about the moment that we enjoy.

Is it a particular sensory experience that thrills you? The sight of a spectacular landscape or of the way the sun catches the sea? The taste of fresh figs? The feel of sand or snow or mud beneath your feet, wind through your hair, succulent leaves brushing against your skin? Is it the sound of birdsong? The smell of the beach at low tide? Or the furious frantic blend of a sprawling city by night?

Or maybe what makes experiences special is something other than the purely sensory. Do you look for those experiences that make you feel a complete connection with those around you? Or those that allow you to be who you really are, unfiltered and unfettered by the presence of another person for miles around?

This is probably the closest I will come in this book to those at best partially useful categories of introvert and extrovert from Myers Briggs, which define you according to whether you get your energy from internal or external sources. Both of those are elements of experience that will help you to understand what something approximating an ideal life might look like. Or at least what kind of experience will be an essential part of it. Introverts will need time alone with their thoughts whatever else they have. Extroverts will need time in a sensorily enriching environment, whatever else they have.

There are other shades that colour the experiences we value. Do you enjoy doing? Or do you prefer just being? That is, are you more active, seeking to interact with the environment you find yourself in, exploring, learning, moving through it? Or do you prefer it to envelop you, to surround and embrace you while you take it in? Along similar lines, do you prefer to be in the audience listening or in front of the audience performing?

And something that will enable you to make choices that are more likely to work as you flesh out the steps that make up this part of your Sustainable Life Goals is figuring out which matters to you more. A series of experiential episodes. Or how you experience life day to day. Are you happy working a 9 to 5 if it means you can share a remarkable adventure with someone you love a few times a year? Or would you rather have a more sensual life day to day in soft clothing, a spacious home, curling up under the finest cotton at night and eating the best food? Or maybe some of you want every day to bring something new, where others value routine.

All of these are about the kind of experience that makes your life meaningful. And the more detail and depth you can bring to this reflection, the more you are likely to build better

Sustainable Life Goals first time around. Though again the fact that you may never have thought in this much depth and will inevitably need to test some assumptions (and will have missed others altogether) emphasises why you need to revisit these reflections regularly.

Section 2 - Understanding why you find it hard to do things

Understanding motivation

Now you have a set of Sustainable Life Goals, the rest of this book is going to be devoted to the most important question of all. How should you live these goals?

But before we get to the concrete steps you can take on a daily basis to make these goals happen, this section addresses something really fundamental. Why are you reading this book? And, assuming that part of the answer is that you are not yet living your ideal life, what has stopped you doing so thus far? Because understanding that is the essential context for making the future different.

The section will fall into two parts. First, I will give you techniques for understanding your motivation more generally. What is it that makes you do some things and not others? What makes you really value some things and not others? And how do these elements - what we might call your directedness - influence the types of strategy that are likely to be more or less effective for achieving your Sustainable Life Goals.

At the end of the section, I will take you back to your Sustainable Life Goals and you can consider how they reflect this directedness - and if needed reconsider them in the light of it. Remember, for the duration of reading this book, your Sustainable Life Goals are provisional. They are a block of marble carefully and through many iterations with tools of increasing fine gauge are being chiselled into a finished sculpture.

Second, we will look at the very specific habits, fears, practices, tendencies, and circumstances that stop you doing the things you want to do. Being aware of them, with brutal honesty, is the first step to figuring out which of them you can overcome, which you can sidestep, and which you will need to learn to live with and adapt accordingly. And we will end the section with strategies and tactics to do that.

Finding your orientation

There are lots of "personality type" models out there. If you're reading a book like this then you're probably familiar with many of them. I won't spend time exploring them - in part because you probably know them already; in part because of what I said in the section about how people make their earnings - I'm not a licensed Myers Briggs practitioner, for example; but mainly because the orientations I do want to focus on are the most practically useful for achieving your life goals.

These orientations are practically useful because they help you to understand why you are drawn to certain ways of living, and why some things motivate you more than others. Understanding these things will help you to create projects and vehicles that are more likely to help you live out your goals because you are more likely to follow the steps they involve.

They will also help you to understand why you find some things harder than others - and to distinguish between those areas you need to work on, those you need to work around, and those you just need to avoid. That will save you a lot of time by helping you not to persist in trying to do things that you're never going to manage, redirecting those energies into things that will work much better for you.

Past and Future

Have you noticed that some people seem to drift through life and others always seem restless? More to the point, have you noticed how some people in each category seem perfectly content? If you are a person who is mentally always on the move, you might wonder how those who never seem to go anywhere - nor demonstrate any sign they want to - seem quite content with their lot. You might even wonder whether they are lying to themselves and that one day they will wake up and realise what they have been missing.

But if you are someone who is happy with the life they have built around them, you might look at people who seem to be, for want of a better phrase, perpetual fidgeters with life and wonder why they can't just breathe, look around them, and realise what they already have.

The answer lies in part in the way people orient themselves in relation to time. Discovering your own orientation on this axis is a key part of understanding what kind of activities in life are likely to satisfy you in the long run.

The key lies in this simple question. Suppose you are imagining a scene from your ideal life. Now zoom in. Are you looking back to something you would like to recapture? Or are you looking ahead to a future you want to create? To put the question slightly differently, when it comes to things as they are now, are you preserver or a disrupter?

The answer will depend on a lot of what has happened so far in your life. But again, the purpose here isn't to offer therapy. It's to offer insight. And through that insight to help you understand what is most likely to form part of your pursuit of your ideal life. This matters, for example, when it comes to deciding how to frame infrastructure goals. If you are a preserver, looking to the past or a continuation of the present, you are more likely to want security from your physical shelter and your finances, and to want to spend time nurturing existing relationships. If you are a disrupter, someone who believes that something better is "out there" the you are more likely to find happiness in things that offer you flexibility, that bring you into contact with new things and new people, with work that is varied.

The Barriers We Face

The second kind of orientation that can have a major impact on our lives derives from the kind of barriers we have faced in life. That is, what are the things that have, in the past, stopped us doing the things we wanted to do? And were we able to overcome those barriers?

Our answers to these two questions will colour how we face challenges in the future. But they will also tend to shape how we see our position in the world and our ability to change it. This matters, because these are beliefs that we think have a fixed basis in reality. We generalise them into universal principles. And that can either leave us frustrated when we confront a problem we believe we should be able to solve but can't; or failing to tackle issues that we could solve because we believe them to be insoluble.

Internal or External?

In the past, when we have set out to do something and not been able, what was it that stood between us and our goals? Or, because that is probably too complex a question for any of us to answer, what is it that we believe kept us from our goals? Was it something inside us or something outside us?

Classic examples of an internal barrier would be levels of physical skill needed to compete at or win an event we had marked out for success, like a 400m run. It could also be the skill we need to enroll in a programme or the knowledge we need to pass an exam. Each of these things constitutes a potential barrier to something we've set our heart on.

Each of those same dreams might also have involved an external barrier. Perhaps the nearest place that organised 400m races when you were a sporty kid desperate to run and win medals was 10 miles away. Perhaps the only athletics club met the same time you needed to be home to care for a parent.

Hard Barrier or Soft Barrier?

As well as being internal or external, barriers we have faced in the past will have either been (or been experiences as at the very least) hard or soft

Hard barriers are ones we cannot overcome. An example of this would be setting a goal to run a mile in under 3 minutes. Something that is simply, in the world right now, not possible. We can also experience things as hard limits that we are not able to overcome as a result of circumstance. Imagine a 4 year-old child watching the Winter Olympics and wanting to become a junior cross country skier. But imagine they live somewhere it never snows, where there are no indoor facilities, and their parents say, "Sorry, we're not moving." This can happen at school as well with teachers who repeatedly say, "No, you're not doing that."

Soft barriers, on the other hand, or specifically barriers that we have experienced as soft, are the ones we have overcome. Because we've got past them we know they're not fixed. To follow from the last paragraph, imagine the would-be winter Olympian had parents whose jobs were relatively flexible and said, "OK, Kid, we can see how much you want this. Let's move somewhere snowier." Or the kid whose teachers always say no who says in return, "Forget this for a lark," and starts taking a detour each morning and instead of arriving at school arrives at the library where they study what they really wanted to all along, just long enough to get the skills they needed to start their own small business doing that thing.

How you experience barriers when you're younger is by and large a matter of circumstance and happenstance. But it will have a huge impact on how you perceive barriers you face later in life. And how you see the world and the way people are able to move through it in general. This can leave you well- or ill-equipped to deal with the barriers you actually face. It can provide you with what looks to others like the tenacity and resilience you need to persist and succeed despite social convention; or it can leave you lacking confidence and hope. It can also leave you surprised when a hard external barrier fails to bend to your will.

As I've said many times already, what matters is reflecting and understanding why you believe what you do about the world. Because that can help you to see the potholes such a worldview can create before you fall into them and wonder how you get out. For example, if you have experienced soft internal barriers, you may be ill-prepared for hard external ones and as a result need to be on the lookout to avoid fruitless quests. Likewise if you have experienced many hard external barriers, you may assume that all is doomed and miss out on things you could have achieved by exercising your agency.

Blockers

Understanding the things that have stood between you and your goals in the past is a vital part of ensuring you build a way of working that does its best to avoid both those issues and the biases and trauma that arise from them in the future.

But just as it is important to create projects and vehicles that sit below your Sustainable Life Goals so that you start each day with specific actions you can take that will enable you to live the life you want, so it is important to be really specific about some of the things you know will make it hard to do those things.

I shouldn't have to say this again because it is the common theme of this whole book. But this will only work if you are absolutely honest with yourself. And if you reflect as deeply as possible, not stopping with superficial answers but following the trail of "why"s until you reach the real truth.

There are many things that stop us doing what we know they should do. I have called these "blockers." Essentially, finding out what your blockers are gives you a constant to do list that sits alongside your Sustainable Life Goals. Like a service checklist for a car, it's your job to ensure that you keep these blockers at bay. Eliminate them if you can. And where you can't eliminate them, find workarounds.

The perfect vs the practical

Let's be really practical on that last point. Life happens. And you are who you are. And sometimes even if you can fix something, doing so would take more resources than working around it by simply finding another way to do what you want. And if we're going to get the most from our lives, pragmatism has to overrule perfectionism. That, in itself, is the first blocker and solution for most of you!

It's amazing how many people I know who have the quotation, "don't let the perfect be the enemy of the good" printed out and pinned somewhere they can see it every day. It's also amazing how many of these people never quite seem to have internalised it.

Indeed, I could write a whole book on inspirational quotations and the role they play. Like most people, I have pages filled with them - in my journal, on my wall, in a special Google doc (and by special I am using the standard terminology meaning, "stored in a place that I have to spend half an hour searching to find"). Looking at quotations that state principles we want to live by can be really important. But knowledge is what you have learned in order to use it, not just to recall it. A quotation that hangs on your wall, even one you have memorised, is no use if you don't work it into your life and live by it. I prefer a tattered worksheet that helps me to change my behaviour to a beautifully presented poster every time.

The most important thing about perfectionism can be summed up in another famous quotation, from the prayer of St Francis of Assisi:

"God, give us grace to accept with serenity
the things that cannot be changed,
Courage to change the things which should be changed,
and the Wisdom to distinguish the one from the other."

Living in Longhand

What makes this so wise is that it acknowledges the difference between what we can and should try to do (which is where even what may seem like perfectionism can be warranted in the right context - and the purpose of this section is to help you work out what that context is), and those things we neither can nor should try to do (which is where even what may seem like laziness or lack of positive thinking can be warranted in the right context - and again it is the purpose of this section to give you the tools to work out what that context is).

Many of the most important self-improvement processes and principles are simply variations on this centuries-old wisdom. Especially productivity techniques. At root, anything that urges you to double down on those things where you can make a real difference and not to obsess over those areas where you would not be using your time or your talents to best effect is based on this same idea.

And at its most fundamental of course, what this simple prayer asks for is what we have been saying all along. Honesty with yourself.

The traits of ineffective goal pursuing

Let's take a deeper dive. These are some of the most common forms of "blocker" to look out for. Not all of these will apply to everyone, but they are a great starting point if you want to understand what kind of things might stop you pursuing your goals. I will take a look also at how you might start to work around or against some of these. But ultimately, the key to that will be personal to you.

People pleasing

This is the one that almost certainly does most harm to most people. And what makes it so damaging is that it intersects with so many things we are brought up to believe are valuable.

Most of us will do at least some things because we care for people and we know that doing those things will make them happy. Most of the time this is something relatively inconsequential like wearing the outfit we don't really like the next time we see the relative who gave it to us, or showing up in the rain to support a friend on their first half marathon because we know seeing a supportive face a mile from the line will help get them through.

Some of the time, these things are repeated, even when we don't really have the time or energy. Like calling someone the same time every Saturday morning because we know they value it. Or carrying on following an interest because our partners want us to share it with them.

Living in Longhand

These are all things that come from motivations that society values deeply. Compassion, consideration, altruism, friendship. These are good things. And to go back to the previous section, they deepen relationships.

On the other hand, how often have you found yourself in the middle of a project you hate; or at an event you would give anything to be able to snap your fingers and leave; or sitting at a meeting watching a roomful of people who seem to be getting something that you are somehow missing. You're exhausted, miserable, and brought up suddenly short by the realisation, "Why am I doing this?"

And how often is that followed by a train of thought that includes the question, "Who am I doing this for?"

Worse still, even if it turns out you are doing this to provide for those closest to you, how often would really honest reflection have led you to conclude that maybe they would be just as happy at least, maybe greatly more so, if you contributed materially less (or, quite probably, differently) but were able to enjoy that contribution more, to share it with them?

But so much of the time, this isn't even about doing something less enjoyable now for the sake of yours and your loved ones' benefit later. Instead, we slip into the habit of saying yes. Because saying yes to things is easier than finding reasons to say no. Because we want people to think well of us without asking ourselves why we want that. Because one of the real reasons we want people to like us is the same as the reason we believe we should say yes when we are asked to do something we don't want to do. And that is, because society tells us we should. Social convention has distilled in us the idea that there is a moral value to saying yes to people. Or rather, that there is a morally negative quality to saying no. Because saying no is selfish and selfishness is bad.

Saying no to things that actively detract from where we want to be in life, and which offer nothing in return, is one of the most important skills we can learn. But it's one of the hardest for those of us who need to learn it most. Because we feel the weight of social convention that we've learned over the years. And that often creates vast reserves of guilt. We also feel that we are personally disappointing the people we want to please. And we can feel as though one of our sources of feeling valued or needed has been turned off.

How you learn to say no will depend on what makes it so hard for you right now. If it is just a matter of never having spent the time reflecting on how you spend your time and emotional resources to notice that many of them are being funneled into the wellbeing of others and not your own, that's the easiest to solve. Because the first step for everyone is to take that time to examine those things.

The process for that examination is a similar kind of questioning as we have been advocating throughout. Use "why?" as a set of chisels that takes you in finer and finer detail from the block of marble to the final sculpture.

Start with the raw information. Keep a journal of everything you do for a week. Break things down activity by activity. For each of those activities - whether that's preparing food, walking the dog, travelling to work, reading a book, watching TV, spending time online, make a note of how it made you feel. Make a note of the goal or goals in your portfolio you think it contributed to. And make a note of why you think you were doing it ("just because" or "I don't know" or "why not?" is absolutely fine at this stage!).

You can colour code this if it works for you. Maybe separately you can use squared paper with a square to represent each 30 minute chunk of the day (as I say, for a week only - unless this really suits you and comes naturally it won't be sustainable - though for some of you it might be). That way you will have an instant visual cue as to what's noticeably overrepresented. And what's absent. One way of doing this really effectively that can also be fun is to use different coloured Lego bricks to build a 3 dimensional colour map of how you spend your time. It's also something you can keep on your desk that might start some interesting conversations.

After a week of doing this, you should be able to look back and get a sense of the underlying factors that determine how you are using your time. Are you nourishing yourself? Nourishing others? Having fun? Assuaging guilt? Trying to "do the right thing"? Clocking up hours at work without purpose? Drifting? Worrying about and trying to avoid things in the future? And you will also get a sense of how it's making you feel. Satisfied? Resentful? Bored? Lonely? Panicked that your life is passing you by? Helpless? Powerful? Happy? Anxious?

Once you know where you are starting out from, you will have a far better idea of those things you need to do more of, and those things you need to do less of. Specifically for this section, you will get a picture of the things you need to say no to more often.

It's an exercise that will reveal where you start in relation to many of the things we'll be looking at in this section. But for now, have a close look at those particular situations in which trying to please someone else led you to spend time and resources doing something that didn't take you closer to where you want to be in life.

There are three approaches you can take once you have identified the situations in which you are most likely to people please.

First is the hardest. But the one that will be most freeing. And that is learning to say no. Protecting your boundaries so that your most valuable resources are spent pursuing the things you most value. Put like that it sounds simple. What a waste of the most precious commodities you have - your time and your bandwidth - to spend them on things that aren't central to what you want most in life. People pleasing is a really slippery habit. You have already identified that "keeping (insert names) happy" is not part of your Sustainable Life Goals. Yet by people pleasing you act as though it were.

That is the first key step to take. Realising that you say yes to these things not because they are vitally important for your life goals. But for some other reason. They *feel* like the most important thing in the world. But now you have identified that it is only a feeling, and one that misrepresents the truth, you can start to strip it of its power.

The things you do to "please people" are not about building relationships. Nor are they about making a positive impact on the world. That is the second key realisation. If they were about those things, then you wouldn't feel resentful. Or, rather, if they are about nurturing relationships and making a positive impact *and* you feel resentful about doing them, then maybe relationships and impact aren't central to your

Sustainable Life Goals like you thought they were. Maybe you weren't as brutally honest as you thought you were being when you drew up your list. In which case be glad you've found that out now, and go back and remove them!

Now that you've established what your motivations for doing these things are not, you can get to the heart of what they are. And you will probably find they are a combination of things we will look at in the next subsections, all of which make saying "no" easier: guilt, lack of self-worth, lack of confidence, and uncritical acceptance of social convention.

The second strategy is to avoid situations in which you know you won't be able to say "no." That sounds like a cop out. But it's not. Often it's a really practical step to take. It's basically working with a principle that's well known in behavioural science. If temptation is all around you, you are more likely to give in to it. If you have sugary drinks on your kitchen counter you are more likely to be overweight than if you don't because you just reach for the drink rather than getting water from the tap. So if you want to lose weight, one of the first things to do is not to have sugary snacks lying around. Make it harder to do the things you don't want to do. And not having to use willpower to avoid things but instead redressing your environment frees up mental bandwidth to do the things that really matter to you - because few things eat bandwidth quite as fast as exercising willpower.

The final approach you can take is what I call value extraction. It's an approach I try to take whenever there are things I can't avoid doing that don't directly help me pursue my Sustainable Life Goals. It involves exactly what it sounds like. If you have to do something, then get what you can from it. Use it to gain a new skill that you can then transfer to another area of your life. I developed a system of journaling that works for my ADHD this way after decades of trying and failing with journaling systems that apparent (neurotypical) experts claimed worked for anyone. I consistently struggled in my day job with forgetting meetings, with important but not urgent tasks, and with keeping track of different projects at the same time. To get my line manager off my back I needed to find a system that would enable me to manage the dull minutiae of my day job well enough to, well, keep my manager off my back. But I realised that these problems also existed in the parts of my life I was passionate about. So I set about creating a journaling system that would do what it needed to at work, and by also helping me in the things that mattered to me would indirectly contribute to my Sustainable Life Goals, even though in theory doing it meant spending valuable time doing busywork which would otherwise take me further from where I wanted to be.

At a more general level, I have been able to extract some value from these otherwise time and resource taking tasks by using them to help me work on a more mindful approach to tasks in general. When your mind isn't free enough to wander because the task at hand won't quite permit it, it can be helpful to stay absolutely in the moment, focused only on the keystroke or equivalent you are performing now.Being able to do that, forgetting the wider context to an extent that the world outside the mechanics of the action I am engaged in might as well not exist has helped immensely with repetitive aspects of tasks that really are valuable to me. Like keeping going in the later stages of an ultra marathon.

Lack of self-worth

We usually do things because we think we should, or because we think it will make others we don't really care about (and who certainly don't care about us) pleased: because we fail to value ourselves fully.

So many of us don't consider ourselves valuable enough that it is worth spending the time doing things that would nurture us. We are socialised into believing that other people are more valuable than we are, that pursuing our dreams should take second place to supporting the dreams of others. And this devaluing tends to be highly gendered, and layered with issues around class. It also manifests in (also highly gendered) expectations around care and parenting. Your children come first - the moment you are a parent your children's dreams eclipse your own.

As a result, several things happen. Many of us never truly develop the belief that our dreams matter. If no one has told us that we should pursue the things that enrich us, it can be hard to develop the belief that it's OK to do so, or that we have a right to expect or at least pursue a certain amount of fulfilment in our lives. This can apply especially when we grow up with dreams outside the regular.

And the pursuit of other people's dreams doesn't fulfil us either because that pursuit comes not from a belief that our satisfaction in life comes from impact and relationship but instead from duty. So we resent rather than enjoy any positive things that might result.

Overcoming this socilaisation is hard. A first step can be to realise that there is an irrational logic behind it. If you believe that everyone's dreams matter but your own, or even that the dreams of someone close to you matter more than your own, consider that person's perspective. If your belief were based on the kind of rational principle that those who socialise us to think like this drum into us ("other people matter more," for example) then to that person, your dreams matter more than theirs. So while you were living for them they would be living for you. If that were the case, something a little more recognisably healthy than your endless self-sacrifice might be the result (though arrived at in a somewhat confusing way). You would certainly have to develop a certain self-worth, because to the other person you really do matter. You have worth, even if not to you.

The sacrifice that is demanded of parents for their children is even more irrational, because it perpetuates a story in which no one ever gets to enjoy life. Your duty is to sacrifice your happiness for that of your children. But then their duty is to sacrifice themselves for the children of their own. And so on. Forever. And in this cycle of sacrifice, whose children actually get to be happy on their own terms and not simply because they've "done their duty" (which they haven't done anyway because that duty was focused not so much on raising their children but on raising them for happiness: which they obviously don't attain)? Nobody's so. But if we were to imagine a situation in which someone, down the line, really does get to be happy, without guilt, the whole chain collapses and the original parent, you, told that you should sacrifice yourself, is actually permitted happiness of their own too.

A lack of infrastructure

For many of us there is one very simple thing preventing us pursuing the life we dream of. We lack the resources to do so. These resources could be financial, they could be time, they could be geographical lack of access; or they might be skills, or opportunity, or support.

This is the reason infrastructure goals are so central to your Sustainable Life Goals. Because the main way to solve this problem is to expand the resources available to you. And the first part of that is understanding what resources you need in order to live the life you desire.

It was important for us to tackle that issue - how to quantify, and then get more, resources - before we looked at the alternative way of solving the same problem: modifying the way you pursue your goals to fit the resources available to you. Because most of the time, changing your goal isn't a fully satisfying answer. Or at least not a simple one. Because it can lead to resentment on the one hand and missed opportunity on the other.

That said, continuing to chase resources that we are never going to attain, or are very unlikely to attain, can be even more soul-destroying. And a recipe for an unsatisfied life. If there are ways you can work either with what you have or what you can more easily obtain while you put yourself in a place where you're open to opportunities to get more then you might find more satisfaction over the span of a lifetime than continuing to chase what you'll never reach.

Working out if it's worth taking this approach involves something you will have become good at by now. Using "why" (and to an extent here, "what?") to dig down. When you look at your Sustainable Life Goals, and what they provide you, why have you listed the exact things you have? What is it about them that gives you the thing you're looking for? What exactly is that thing? What else might provide it?

For example, if it matters to you to experience new places and new experiences, that might initially mean something that requires considerable time and financial resources. You might have imagined a life of travelling - swimming in coral seas, walking the Machu Picchu Trail, skiing in New Zealand.

And here I want to make an important aside that a lot of people who advocate "reframing" fail to make. I am not suggesting you "settle for less" than what you originally dreamed of. I am asking whether, if those things are not possible right now (it's actually a particularly useful exercise if they *are* possible because then you will be able to explore alternatives with a fully open mind), by digging down and discovering the motivation and genuine experiential desire behind those things you always imagined, you might be able to achieve the same goals by different means. Maybe the alternatives could lead to what you had imagined originally. And maybe they will envelop you in a world you hadn't originally imagined but turn out to love.

To repeat, anyone who tells you that you can just get the same effect by doing something cheaper probably either hasn't done enough reflection - or is just trying to get you to lie to yourself. And those are the only two things I will ever really talk about as "sins" in this book. It may be that you really can be just as satisfied with something inexpensive. But maybe you can't. And realising you can't won't get you the money you need. But it will give you genuine information with which you can make better decisions about prioritising your time; or even a way to start the process of acceptance that can lead to avoiding resentment down the line.

Back, as it were, to dreams of swimming among the coral. My ADHD means that new experiences are essential to my enjoyment of life. And while I'm not an "adrenaline junkie" I do find the unfamiliar incredibly comforting. In my 30s, at the height of the budget flight boom, my spouse and I satisfied that need by travelling round Europe on a shoestring, at one point visiting 23 countries in a year. We were even on the cover of Woman's Own, with the byline "We travelled the world for the price of a cup of coffee. Here's how you can too!"

More recently I have discovered trail running as a way of pushing new experiences both internally, as my body transformed from 19 stone and unable to walk across the car park without stopping for breath to just under 12 stone and running 100 kilometre ultramarathons, and externally as I get to move through spaces I would never have the chance to see if my body couldn't do what it now can. My Sustainable Life Goals included exploring the world through movement. And by "the world" I really meant the whole world.

One of the things that happened with the restrictions on mobility that came into force in 2020 was that a lot of the things I had imagined would give my life purpose on a relatively stable basis disappeared, as they did for everyone, overnight. One of the things that was interesting about how this impacted the ultra running community is that where people had used races to create the structure in their calendar and help them see the world, now they went all in on a different approach. In 2020 and 2021 in particular runners across the globe pursued local, FKTs: the fastest known times for travelling along recognised trails. Ally Beaven's book Broken provides a great account of many of these epic runs.

What lockdowns did for me was to make me inventive about how I used the very limited circle of space in the few miles around my office in Oxford. I'm used to getting on the bus to do any kind of meaningful trail running, heading to the Ridgeway, which I can join either East or South West of the city about an hour's ride away. Despite having been based in Oxford for more than 30 years I had never realised there are actually plenty of not only steep but steep and muddy and moderately sustained trails to be explored all within a mile of the ring road.

During lockdown I made a conscious choice to discover the green spaces in and around Oxford that had been previously hidden to me. And to find interesting ways to run around and between them. I found more than 20 parks and nature reserves in the city centre itself. I created loops of trails connecting them. And then ways to join the hills surrounding the city into loops of 20, 30, 50 kilometres and more during which I could push my navigation and exploration skills and spend much of the time oblivious to the fact I was in a city at all. And when I was back on tarmac, I began trying out techniques from parkour to make the journeys more interesting. I even played with setting mental challenges like memorising cards or solving a Rubik's cube when I reached certain checkpoints on the way.

What I opened up was a whole new way of moving through a city whose potential I thought I had exhausted long since. And doing that opened up the possibility of creating more tiny acts of exploration that I've been playing with ever since. They are not even micro adventures, so much as nano adventures that can transport me to the edge of my knowledge and potential in as little as a lunch hour, simply by going through a door or down an alley or up a flight of stairs or across a bridge I'd always passed by.

It would be easy to turn the point into something trite about finding contentment within the confines of the hand one has been dealt. That's not what I want to do. The human spirit is restless. It longs to explore the new and the familiar. And pretending to oneself that limiting circumstances don't matter is to deny something fundamental. Then again, failing to accept there are some things you cannot change, and some you can't change for now, isn't helpful either. Necessity may not be the mother of invention, but what it can be is a very good prompt for getting to the truth behind your dreams. It can help with the process of asking why. And sometimes what it tells you will enable you to find ways of pursuing your dreams that turn out to be possible with the cards you have.

Fomo

Fear of missing out, FOMO, is for many of us the main reason we keep saying yes to things about which we end up saying, "Why did I say yes to this?" as we look at our endlessly packed schedule and all the things we want to do but can't.

The key to working out how to say yes to the right things but not to everything, "just in case," is having a much clearer understanding of what it is we want from the things we say yes to.

Before I look more closely at this, it's important to look at the role that serendipity plays in our lives and the opportunities it presents, so that we avoid throwing the baby out with the bath water as it were.

One of the things I advocate for a lot in this book is a more intentional life. That we notice the extent of the decisions we make every day. But that level of intentionality has dangers, and the intersection with FOMO is the best place to illustrate this danger. In this brief section, I want to explain how to avoid saying yes to so many things we later regret simply out of FOMO while not only not missing out on opportunities by not being in the right pace at the right time, but increasing our exposure to and ability to capitalise on those opportunities.

I'll start by giving an illustration of serendipitous opportunity and one of damaging FOMO from my own experience.

I often say that almost every opportunity that came my way happened as a result of sticking my hand up when people asked for volunteers and then seeing what happened. That, of course, is only partially true.

In the late Noughties and early 2010s, before I turned more to non-fiction, I spent a lot of time writing and performing poetry. I was part of an incredibly vibrant and exciting performing scene that spanned London, Oxford, and the South of England. It was a time when poetry slams were on the rise and spoken word was increasingly gathering attention beyond basements, student common rooms, and experimental black box theatres.

Within the space of a few years, during this heady time, I was able to go from a random person sitting in an office with too many dreams and not enough inhibition to performing at the Royal Albert Hall, taking my own troupe of performers, The New Libertines, to venues across the country, and even putting on festivals.

And almost all of this came about because I put my hand up at the right moments. Every time I turned up to poetry slams I performed. And I'd go to any event I could find, anywhere I could find it, every night of the week - even if there were only two people and a cat in the audience. And I became an incredibly vocal blogger and equally loud on social media, constantly telling people what I thought was wrong with the poetry world - why it was selling out, why events needed more pizazz, why we needed more impresarios in poetry like the Jay Joplings and Nick Serotas who had driven the explosion of conceptual art.

And when people inevitably challenged me by asking if I thought I knew the answers, why didn't I do something about it - I said, OK I will. And I did. I went around book shops and cafes and art galleries and night clubs and fringes telling anyone who'd listen I was going to revolutionise the literary world. Or at the very least, if they gave me an evening then I could put on a show that would bring people to their venue, give them a chance to sell drinks and whatever else they had on offer, and give them the chance to get in at the start of nothing less than a new movement.

And it worked. Most of them said yes. And I put on a show the likes of which they hadn't seen before. Many of the poets who were part of The New Libertines went on to Edinburgh, highly acclaimed solo shows, bestselling written as well as spoken word careers. I was a mediocre poet. A really quite good performer. But my skills were spotting talent and selling people on a very particular vision - a vision of a new and better way of doing things. And once I had sold that vision sufficient for them to say, OK, what have you got, I used that eye for talent, refusal to accept conventional wisdom, and ability to spot the need and possibility for the innovative to show them another world - one that captivated them. And their punters!

It was an approach I've taken all my life. It was how I ended up captaining the school general knowledge and bridge teams (yes, I am aware putting that on my CV is "not the hot take I think it is"); it's how I pitched up to something called the Mind Sports Olympiad when it launched in 1997 and as a result ended up as World Intelligence Champion and 4 times Creative Thinking World Champion. It's even how I ended up with my own creative thinking start-up.

If I hadn't taken on a completely scattergun approach, I would never have had the opportunities I did in the poetry world. It gave me some incredible experiences and some remarkable memories. But there came a point where the scales tipped.

A few years into this life, I started to realise I was feeling frustrated. It was one of the first times I really started to reflect on why I was so dissatisfied with a life that I'd thought was deeply satisfying. The first thing I noticed was something that would become a theme. And something that is, I guess, inevitable for someone whose most saleable talent lies in being an impresario. Actually thinking about my life as a "poet," an analysis of how I actually spent my time revealed I was spending almost none of it writing, performing, or rehearsing. I was spending all of it putting on a showcase for other poets. Instead of writing I was spending hours reading other people's work. People had realised I could open doors and I was getting more and more requests to be part of the New Libertines troupe, more and more requests to spend "just 5 minutes" reading and reviewing other people's work.

Doing those things would, a few years before, have been the way I put my hand up and found opportunity. Now they had become the things keeping me from opportunity.

And this is the key to the difference between taking opportunity and endlessly doing things simply out of FOMO.

Once you have identified your Sustainable Life Goals, then creating ways to put yourself in situations where you have opportunities to pursue them is a valuable strategy. Going to events, taking part in forums, joining groups - all of these things are part of creating networks, developing skills, demonstrating what you can do - the kind of things that push doors open for you. Saying "yes" early on to as many of those doors as you are able to walk through - especially if you are not 100% sure yet on the detail of the projects and vehicles that will make up your pursuit of a Sustainable Life Goal - that's a way to explore possibilities.

But this is where keeping on monitoring is part of staying on track. Because unless "participating in the local poetry community" or the equivalent IS the thing that makes up your sustainable life goal, then the things that bring opportunity today may well bring stagnation tomorrow. And the things that were unimaginable yesterday may be what is essential for opportunity today.

We will look in the next section at how to use projects and vehicles within our Sustainable Life Goals to establish what tasks to do each day in order to live the lives we want to live. But the point here is that it is not the individual actions alone that matter. The lie that FOMO tells us is that it is the individual actions that matter to our futures and not the reason for those actions. This is a lie that's easy to fall into from habit. On a day to day level we don't, and we don't need to, focus only on the long term or the bigger picture. We achieve the bigger picture by getting on with the day to day. But it is the bigger picture that matters. And that bigger picture, broken down into the actions that will achieve it, is our primary weapon against FOMO.

Distant elephants and undigested frogs

We rarely (sometimes; but rarely) take things on that we know we're not going to be able to manage to do. Most of the things we say we'll do seem perfectly reasonable when we say we'll do them.

So why do so many things, when their time comes, feel so utterly overwhelming?

The answer lies with a pair of animals. The phrases, "beware distant elephants" and "learn how to swallow a frog" (it's interesting that one of the keys to doing this ties the two together in the punchline to the question, "how do you eat an elephant?") aren't mine, but I hope I can offer some insights into the meaning behind them that will help you avoid these blockers.

Let's start with distant elephants. The phrase seems to have originated with productivity guru Kevin Kruse. I recommend you read his book 15 Secrets Successful People Know About Time Management for its original meaning and his advice.

But what I want to talk about is its goal setting context, and how it can help you to use Sustainable Life Goals as ways to choose what to say no to. And also, perhaps even more important, I want to show you how your increased understanding of the cumulative effect of seemingly small things, gained from our earlier work on Sustainable Life Goals, can be a very powerful analytic tool that will enable you to find it easier to say no to things that might seem really trivial at the time but would end up having a large detrimental effect on your progress if you let them slip through the net.

The "distant elephants" name refers to something we will all recognise. Even the largest objects, when viewed from far enough away, seem tiny. When it comes to commitments, it doesn't really matter how much work is actually going to be involved in doing something. If we are asked for our commitment far enough in advance we will often say yes because it's hard to get into a head space where we can properly imagine just how much of a tailspin such an undertaking will put us in a week out from the task.

For many of us, this might be signing up for a marathon when the race entries open. Or agreeing to give a talk for a works conference. Or saying in the winter that you'll spend the summer holidays stripping out the old rotten floors and putting new laminate in. We think, "That sounds like a good idea. It kind of needs doing. Why not?" then reach for the remote and forget about it for months. Then, when we get the email joyfully telling us it's just a month till race day, or the note from the tech department asking if you have slides and if so could you send them over, we look a our diaries, do a quick calculation of available time, and on arriving with a hefty negative number, go into a panic.

Approaching life from the perspective of Sustainable Life Goals means both a more intentional and a more holistic way of tackling decisions about what to say yes to. A way that will help to avoid this kind of panic by design.

What I mean here by intentional is a conscious calculation. Conscious, that is, as opposed to the reflexive, "yes, I'll do that" that we sometimes give as an answer. And also as opposed to taking on commitments as an emotional response driven by fear or guilt - the kind of response we've been talking about previously in this chapter. Instead, when we consider whether to take something on, we are calculating which of our Sustainable Life Goals it will contribute to.

But conscious calculation also means, to return to our leitmotif, being honest. Being honest about the resources that something would take to complete, even if it's something a long way in the future. And honest about whether we are equipped to do it. Do we have not only the time, but the skills, the access to equipment, the financial resources, all the infrastructure that such an undertaking would involve? And if we don't, how easy or hard would it be to acquire that infrastructure? And what would taking steps to acquire it add to the resource cost of the undertaking itself.

Finally, and most important of all in this context, being intentional means understanding the cumulative impact of the things we do. In its simplest terms, that means saying "Sure, I could do that. But what else have I got on? And even if I don't have anything else in the diary right now, what am I going to have to say no to if I take this on?" Because what makes far-off undertakings so difficult isn't so much this task or that task on the list of things you have to do. It's the fact that so many of them all line up at once.

That is, the problem is the cumulative effect of the elephants beyond each elephant itself. Indeed, the cumulative effect can mean that even small undertakings can have a disproportionate impact on our lives if they are part of a cumulative overload. It is this cumulative effect that Sustainable Life Goals work with in a positive way to create better lives. These goals are not about one or two major events but about the fact that lots of ongoing things across many areas of our lives come together to bring our life richness. What the distant elephant phenomenon warns us is that the same principle can work to overwhelm us if we're not careful.

Fully understanding the power of the cumulative is our secret weapon in making sure that we not only know but use the techniques for avoiding overwhelm. It's easy to say to yourself that you know you should block out the time in your distant future with as much care as you do your time next week. But if you don't really believe that it matters, you'll still find yourself thinking that one more little thing won't hurt.

Key among those overwhelm-avoiding techniques will be using the framework of projects, vehicles, and what I call "jacquard training," which is the focus of the final section of this book. These will provide you with very effective ways to ensure that you set out to work on a very limited number of your Sustainable Life Goals with an extra level of depth at any one time while undertaking a maintenance level of work at most times on most of the others. It will provide you with specific mechanisms for that deep work, which in turn you will break down into day to day tasks. And once that framework is in place, a key part of which will be sacrosanct empty space for "whatever life throws at you," your diary will become blocked out even to the tiniest extra thing.

Phrases around "swallowing frogs" are also not mine, but the truth behind those phrases is something we encounter every day. Some goals feel forever out of reach not because we lack skills or infrastructure related to those goals, or even because we lack time. They are out of reach because achieving them would involve doing at least one thing we simply cannot bring ourselves to do.

It is here that theory and practice butt up against each other. Or rather, it's at this point any theory about productivity and how to "make best use" of the time and resources we have will fail if it doesn't acknowledge that the thing employing time and resources in this way is not a machine but a human being. And human beings are complicated by psychology and emotions - as we've already seen with FOMO and guilt.

The reason why some tasks (the "frogs" of the saying) seem "too big" or "too difficult" for us to do/swallow them boils down to a human factor.

Let's look at an example many of us will have encountered. Asking our manager for a pay rise. If we need more money in order to live the life we dream of, this might well be the first thing that comes to mind, and in many cases it will be a necessary step to take. If you break that down into the actions involved, there will rarely be many steps in the process that are beyond someone's technical skills or the infrastructure they have at hand. Yet many people would nod in recognition if you told them that after weeks you still found yourself staring at a blank email or spent hours looking at the telephone like it was something mysterious but had come no closer to using it.

There are many reasons why some things feel as though they're simply impossible. Not that the task itself is so big that we lack the perspective to divide it into small enough steps for us to take the first of those (that's the "eating elephants" pop psychology not the "swallowing frogs" one). Rather, the task is in and of itself too difficult for us. Again, it's not that we lack skills in the general sense. Most of us know how to compose an email. But it's the content of that email that creates the barrier. The problem is not the theory but the practice.

I want to look at three reasons why we find these tasks hard. As before, the main reason for doing that is awareness. It may be that awareness is the first step to then overcoming the blocker and being able to perform the task. But I'm not one of those gurus who'll shout at you and call you weak if you don't "just do the thing." Sometimes that would be the best solution for the long term and the pay off would outweigh the difficulty of getting to that position (it will largely depend on which of the reasons we're going to look at applies to you). Sometimes it wouldn't. I take a much more pragmatic approach.

I recognise that sometimes it can actually be more effective to find workarounds that avoid putting you in the situation where you feel a complete block. This brings to mind something the legendary climber Alex Honnold says about why it is that he started climbing free solo: that is, without any ropes to keep him attached to the rock face he's climbing, the most dangerous - and often spectacular - form of rock climbing. It was easier, he says, when he first started out, to learn how to climb without a rope than it was to ask someone to climb with him.

That's quite a hard core example, but the principle it illustrates is a sound one. Sometimes when it feels too hard to do something, it's not only simply easier to find a workaround. Doing that can lead you down some really interesting paths.

With that in mind, let's start asking why and looking at the reasons we find some things really hard to contemplate.

First there's embarrassment. This is the one that's probably most rewarding to work on overcoming rather than steering around, because you will develop skills by doing so that will serve you well in many areas.

Embarrassment is quite a broad heading and working out where within that breadth you sit will require more of the brutal honesty you're developing so well. Do you worry about looking a bit daft in front of someone whose opinion you really respect? Or do you have a really deep-seated social anxiety that would need tackling at the root? Are you worried about what your friends would say if footage of you doing the thing found its way onto social media? Or do you have a sizeable base of followers you've built over the years who'd all of a sudden change the way they thought about you? Or a more conventional kind of boss who might take a closer look at your CV?

You might think of all of these as embarrassment, but they are not all equal. And when it comes to the ways (and indeed whether) you might tackle your embarrassment, which kind of embarrassment you experience might change your approach. Again, I'm not here to give detailed psychological advice. But I will illustrate what I mean.

One of the more effective ways of tackling many forms of embarrassment is to take the kind of approach used in cognitive behavioural therapy (CBT). The principle behind CBT is to take an evidence based approach to challenging negative thoughts. It combines exposure to the thing one wants to overcome, for example a fear of heights or nervousness talking to people at parties, with a mental challenge to the thoughts you want to overcome, based in part upon the outcome of that exposure. You went up a tall building, and nothing bad happened. You've spoken to 8 different strangers now, and the world didn't end.

The problem with using CBT in the wrong setting is that sometimes the evidence it relies on isn't there. You might be too embarrassed to approach your manager for a pay rise. But depending on the workplace and the manager, maybe the answer to "what's the worst that can happen?" is that you're next in line for firing. And it's all very well saying "in that case you're better off out" but sometimes, when the landlord wants their rent now and you end up out of a home as well as a job, that kind of response just comes across as trite.

What I'm saying is that if embarrassment is holding you back, the way you tackle your embarrassment needs to be based on, yup, a really honest assessment of the situation.

And that brings us to the second thing that stops us doing things. The stakes involved.

By this, I'm talking about the risk/consequence element of the actions we're thinking about. Some actions, like asking for a pay rise, or even getting in a car and driving to see someone, have a low risk. It's unlikely anything bad will happen. But the consequence, or the hazard as it's sometimes put, is really big. If something does go wrong, it could go wrong really badly. If your manager thinks you're getting above yourself, you could be next up for firing. If you have a crash, you could die.

In everyday life, oftentimes the risk of something bad happening is so low, that however great the consequence might be if it does go bad, we treat it as effectively zero. Some of those times, the risk is a little higher than "effectively zero" but the action that brings the risk is so integral to our lives that our brains smooth over that difference. Getting in a car is one of those. Familiarity and necessity have combined to condition our brain to cancel out any conflicting evidence to the "effectively zero risk" narrative, to the extent that it takes someone very close to us being involved in an accident for us to be jolted out of that, and even then that jolt can often fade.

This is one reason why we will often be shocked by a car accident in the way that news of a plane crash might strike us as dramatic but not shocking. Because for most of us plane crashes are not everyday and necessary, our brains haven't been conditioned. So we recognise that the "effectively zero" element of risk is nonetheless not zero. I would suggest that the reason we perceive greater risk in air travel than car travel is not, as is often supposed, because the dramatic nature of an air crash makes us overestimate its risk, but because the everyday and unavoidable nature of road travel has led our brains to underestimate its risk.

There are other ways in which our brains can lead us into apparently irrational assessments of risk. We can understand the incentive for actions that we find useful to perform daily to be considered less risky than they are, and the selective bias our brains seek out to enable that illusion. But we are also reward-seeking creatures. We value rich and enjoyable lives. For many of us, richness comes in part from activities that have a relatively high risk of a relatively serious consequence.

Of course, in some cases the mechanisms involved in seeking and pursuing behaviour is physiological. Some brains produce or respond to dopamine differently, and that can influence how the brain's acting or inhibiting functionality works. That aside, In cases where richness comes from behaviours that seem to carry a higher risk of higher consequence than many brains are comfortable living with, we work on that barrier by, for example, acquiring a degree of mastery within certain parameters. Building extreme technical proficiency at, say, climbing or diving or skiing, and the repetition involved in doing so, leads the brain into a feeling of security that enables it to become more comfortable over time with riskier and riskier actions.

Of course, that kind of mastery actually does reduce risk in many ways. But often not as much as we think, which is why some activities still have high rates of injury and death. Mastering the techniques of climbing can reduce the risk of making a mistake and falling. But they won't do much to reduce the risk of an avalanche. Mastering meteorology will help with that, but only up to a point.

The brain's ability to become comfortable with risk through repetition, exposure (and sometimes the incentive provided by the way the dopamine system works) can be fatal. In these instances, we can use Sustainable Life Goals as part of a brain-based counterweight. If many things make up our goals in life, then our inability to access most of them (if we were to die in an accident) will be a rational incentive to dial back on our riskier behaviour. Of course, for many who pursue extremely risky behaviour, the very issue is that one goal tends to dominate every other. Not to mention that brains set on pursuing adventure find it very hard to steer off course purely as a result of a rationality they've effectively spent years learning to override.

On the other hand, in many cases, our brains overestimate the risk of a serious negative consequence to an action. And in these cases it can be helpful to remember that it is possible to reacclimatise brains - in this case to bring them more into line with reality.

The third reason why some things seem almost impossible is trauma. The past memory of attempting something similar only to experience a catastrophic result. This is the kind of experience that renders CBT style approaches meaningless. CBT asks, "If you've done this before, did something really bad happen?" In the case of trauma, the answer is, "Yes, thanks for bringing that up!"

There are two ways in which you might continue the approach with more questions. "Was it really that bad?" is one question. And the other is, "Was the bad thing really so likely that it might happen again?"

This continued line of questioning might work for you. It doesn't work for me. One reason that makes it less likely to work than not is that it misses something we have already seen about how experience shapes the brain's responses. Traumatic events leave a deep imprint. They can form what we might think of as habitual responses in a single instance. Undoing that response is just as hard.

The "reality" of an experience when it comes to the subsequent effect on our lives lies in how the brain experiences that event not something rational outside of that experience. Realising, for example, that the scary thing we thought we saw in the middle of the night as a child was the moon-cast shadow of a toy and not a ghost might be a useful starting point for enabling us to sleep with the light off. But the journey will likely still be a long one. And we need to consider whether it's worth starting.

Sometimes confronting the thoughts that prevent us acting as we would like with reason is not only worth it but essential. If you imagine every version of your ideal life containing a life partner, but you are unable to take steps towards a relationship because of past rejection, for example.

But sometimes confronting that block is neither worthwhile nor necessary. And the best way forward is to go around. If you need a pay rise, for example, then maybe instead of figuring out how to approach managers who have repeatedly belittled or even victimised you for similar requests you could as easily figure out how to go freelance.

There are two things that self-help advice in general doesn't emphasise enough, and I want to underline here. And both of them are based in what we might call a confessional approach to self-improvement. The term goes back to obvious religious roots, when a penitent would confess their sins to a priest in order to receive absolution for them, often in return for a penance. This would then enable them to move forward with their lives.

The confessional element has stayed with us. Sigmund Freud's emphasis on confronting truths about one's childhood has perpetuated it. And more recently social media's offering of a platform to anyone with something to say has enabled it.

We are taught many things, such as the importance of being open and honest about our feelings and our experiences, and not keeping things repressed inside us where they lurk waiting to trip us later. What we are taught less is that radical openness and honesty needn't involve a long process of penance and reformation, nor a public confession.

Sometimes, we can go back to that other piece of wisdom with religious origins, the prayer of St Francis. And to a mindful approach. Sometimes what matters is being aware of the trauma that has made some things so hard for us. And, being aware, to acknowledge that and then move on from it by finding ways to work around the difficulty it presents us.

This is very much a mental version of the technique that traceurs, practitioners of parkour, adopt. In order to move through their (literal) surroundings, when traceurs come to an obstacle, they don't stop and try to figure out how to move it. That would be a complete waste of time. These aren't traffic cones or moveable A-signs. They're steel and concrete, with foundations dug into the fabric of the city. The way to move fluidly through such an environment is to train your body to move around and over, and to train your mind to see the unmarked pathways that a body trained in this way can use.

In general too many self-improvement techniques treat too many of the obstacles we face in our lives like traffic cones, movable street furniture that we can pick up and put out of the way. And too few of those obstacles as steel and concrete that we shouldn't be trying to move. And that we wouldn't need to try to move if we were to see the terrain of our inner lives in as many dimensions and with the same flexibility as the traceur sees the terrain of the city stretching before them.

With such an approach, we would spend less of our time training our minds for an essentially impossible task. And more of our time training them to navigate these newly discovered pathways that require not an unreasonable strength but an attainable flexibility and agility.

The other mistake too many self-improvement techniques make is to overplay the importance of persistence. We are regaled with tales of the successful person who tried "one more time", who would never have finally made it had they not kept pushing beyond the point when others moved on.

We hear less about the people who persisted and persisted and pushed one last time, only for that final push to send them into burnout. We hear little about the things that remain undone, the problems that remain unsolved, because people kept knocking at a door that would never open rather than changing tack.

Like all the most important skills, learning when to draw a line under a task or ambition and move on is something that takes much practice. And you will get it wrong. The problem is that society tells us there is a better and a worse way to get the answer wrong to the question, "Should I try once more?"

We are too often led to believe that to try one too many times is an admirable failing and to try one too few times is a shameful one. That the former is heroic, the latter ultimately a matter of laziness. What is stressed less is that to fail by trying one too few times can be the more pragmatic approach. It leaves you with the mental energy to regroup. To ask what went wrong. To seek ways to fix it. And ultimately to assess whether the barrier might be too immovable and a new route might be found. And if it can be, you still have the energy to pursue that new route.

The "try more" doctrine would remind us that when we look back on our lives we will wonder, if we didn't have one more go, what might have happened if we did. It fails to mention the possibly equal regret that we tried too hard too early at the wrong thing and the rest of our life was less than it might have been as a result. It also fails to mention that if, when we stop, we carry out a full and honest analysis before deciding what next, then the regret has no basis in reality. The only thing that we can say would have made "the next time" we did not attempt different is luck. And failure to anticipate an unlikely bout of luck (very different from not putting yourself in the right place for opportunity) is no basis for regret - if it were then we would all spend our last days and most of those before them in mental anguish.

We have spent much time looking in much depth at the things which make it hard for us to act. The reason for this is very simple. It means that when it comes to setting out the steps we need to follow on a daily basis to achieve our Sustainable Life Goals, we will be better equipped. On the one hand we will know in advance which things are likely to cause us the greatest difficulty and can prepare to mobilise resources accordingly. We can even make overcoming some of those barriers a part of our Sustainable Life Goals. On the other hand there will be some things we are able to avoid altogether to save us large amounts of time and energy persisting in pursuing a course that was destined never to work.

We have distinguished between internal and external barriers, and between barriers that are movable with effort and those that are not, meaning we can learn when and how to mitigate and when to accept that we need to change the path we take to move around a barrier. We have become, in doing so,. Like parkour practitioners of the mind.

Now let's turn our attention to the nuts and bolts of pursuing Sustainable Life Goals using this new-found awareness.

Section 3 Creating Concrete Plans

The jacquard principle

Pursuing Sustainable Life Goals requires developing a way of ensuring you can work towards multiple goals at any one time without ever dropping the ball on any one of them. A holistic set of goals requires a holistic way of living, and a holistic way of determining how to act on a day to day basis. Without having such a framework, it becomes almost impossible to avoid losing the big picture in the minutiae of what you are focusing on right now, only to find a few months down the line that you are actually specialising and working towards individual goals. Or you get so overwhelmed by the scope of your Sustainable Life Goals that you are unable to convert them into day to day actions at all.

The system I will outline in this section is designed to provide you with exactly the framework you need to pursue all of your Sustainable Life Goals – without stretching you too thin and leaving you feeling as though you are performing an impossible juggling act; without having constantly to reassure yourself that nothing has been forgotten. It is designed to ensure you never wake up and wonder what you need to do, but at the same time provide the flexibility that will avoid you falling into boredom or pushing back through resistance to the constraint of habits struggling to form. It is designed to work with you and not against you, allowing you to find your own path sometimes over, sometimes breaking down, and sometimes going around the barriers that stand between you and your Sustainable Life Goals.

To introduce this system, we need to talk about one of the interests I picked up when my life took an unexpected turn in my late 20s and I found myself working in a warehouse. Carpets. Specifically, one of the most important techniques devised for the manufacture of carpets, the Jacquard Loom.

These days, anyone outside the world of fabric who hears about the jacquard loom will probably do so because it is one of the very earliest illustrations of the relationship between software and hardware, and understanding how it was used to solve the problem of mass production of patterned fabric is one of the very best introductions to understanding how computers originated and how software enables us to solve exactly that kind of mass production problem by giving a set of instructions - a programme - to a piece of hardware.

The way the jacquard loom uses software is part of what I want to talk about. But I am much more interested in the other part of what it does. In how it produces beautiful, complex-patterned fabric not by dying a plain piece of cloth but by weaving many strands of individually coloured thread into a single work of textile art.

Let me explain briefly how the jacquard loom works. Then we'll see the ways this will help us to think about the principles of pursuing a rounded life. Suppose you want to create a textile with a pattern that has six colours. On a jacquard loom you would start by loading six spools of thread onto the loom, one in each colour. Before you begin weaving, you would load a card that contains what I described a moment ago as the software of the loom. In the earliest jacquard looms, this was a simple punchcard. It encodes the pattern you want to create by telling the loom which colour thread should be stitched at the front at any one moment.

This means you can create any pattern you can think of using those six colours.

The jacquard loom converts the instructions coded into that punchcard into an actual pattern. If the card says "red", the red thread is pulled to the fore; if it says "green", the corresponding thread is selected. And this happens for every single stitch. What makes the jacquard loom even more clever is that while every stitch has a prominent, displayed, colour, the other five threads at that point are still involved. They form the textile's base, the backing that gives it strength and structure, so no cuts are ever made, leaving no frayed ends. Every thread runs continuously from the start to the end of the fabric, sometimes to the front but always contributing to the textile itself.

As you were reading through that, you were probably already thinking how the principle might describe a life of sustainable goals. The key point is that while every goal is always a part of your life, sometimes one will be to the fore, sometimes another. But the overall pattern blends the richness of each. And all of them contribute at every point.

The jacquard system as applied to pursuing your Sustainable Life Goals works by creating a lifestyle in which you are always working towards each of those goals, but only ever have one or two in the foreground.

And like the punchcards that tell the loom which thread to bring to the fore, the jacquard system is built on patterns that enable you to cycle between each of your goals so that each is foregrounded in its turn, and maintained when it is forming the structural integrity of your life in the background.

This system will maximise the "area under the curve" - making the benefit to you in each area you have chosen as high as it can be given everything else you are also doing. It's the lifestyle equivalent of the decathlete who, for the sake of their all around performance, is never so focused that they are the very best at any one thing but has an all around athleticism no specialist can equal.

The next section will introduce the nuts and bolts of how to put this system into practice.

Vehicles, Projects, and tasks

As humans, we relate to the world within different timescales, from the day to day details of what to do from one moment to the next to the geological clock on which continents shift. In this section, I want to focus in on the three timeframes that are most important for motivation, and explore how we can use them to help us develop a programme that ensures we are able to live a rich, rounded life in which we rotate the main focus our activities in such a way that, like a great scene in a film, we enter and leave each at exactly the right moment.

It is essential that as we shift our focus we never think, "Do I have to?" Because we are ready to start and have that familiar surge of adrenaline that comes with something new and exciting. Likewise, whilst we might move on "wanting more" in the very best way, we need to plan so that when it's time to shift again we don't pine to cling on, and we can look back on the most recent period of time and both be pleased with what we have accomplished as a standalone, and satisfied with how it has contributed to our life plan.

The three timescales I want to focus on are the day, the season, and the generation. Let me recap briefly why these are so important.

The Day

The day is the basic unit of time into which our lives are divided. It's the atom as it were. You can get significantly smaller, but it's the level at which most actions we contemplate are self-contained. By that I mean that the things we do, the reasons we do them, and the results we expect to see from them fall into one of two categories.

The first is what we might call "trivial." That is, many of the choices we face on a day to day level have few lasting consequences. Should I wear a black T-shirt or a grey one? Should I have muesli for breakfast or granola? Within certain bounds (maybe it does matter if I wear the death metal T-shirt if I'm visiting a certain kind of person; maybe if I have sausage, bacon, and eggs every day then over time that will have an impact) these things don't matter. The more of them we can automate and the less bandwidth we use on them the better.

The second is what we might call "simple." This is, again, a self-contained action, one that doesn't really include much movement or progression in itself, but nonetheless contributes something significant to an overall journey in our lives. A workout at the gym would fall into this category, or an exercise on Duolingo, or a practice session on the violin, or reading a chapter of a book. Yes, we might get a PR, or we might learn something new, or make breakthrough with our bowing. But the reason we do these things isn't to see that particular progress on that particular day. It's because repeating these actions over longer periods of time is how we make progress on a significant scale.

The Season

The season is the name I use for, as it suggests, periods of around three months, and is based on the cycle of crop planting, growing, and harvesting. It's a time frame within which it is possible to complete a meaningful piece of work if you apply yourself consistently and smartly through that period.

There are many examples in everyday life of using this kind of time period to divide up complete cycles of activity. The most obvious is the academic term. This is the period over which you would learn a complete module, from introduction to end of term paper or exam. Another is the training cycle of an athlete, who might divide the year up into blocks of base training (whether that's endurance or strength) in which the focus is on volume, speed training, in which the emphasis is on adding sharpness, and then competing.

Choices about what to do from day to day within the context of a seasonal cycle are not trivial. That is to say, it matters to the athlete whether their workout is based around strength or speed. It matters to the student whether they read about the French Revolution today or the end of the Roman Empire.

Neither is the decision always simple. It's not enough to repeat the same workout again and again for three months. Because if you do that you will never make progress. So you need to relate what you do today both to what you did in your previous workout and to what you hope to accomplish over the seasonal period.

The generation

This is a slightly more flexible time. It could be anything from three to five to twenty years - to use the examples from the last section that would represent a complete academic course or an athletic career.

This is a period during which you can go from motivated beginner to mastery. Motivated because the horizon is just right for picturing the connection between you as you begin and you as you become, joined together by a succession of steps you can imagine yourself taking. And mastery because you have sufficient time for the power of compounding to take effect, building on consistent practice. Not to mention time to explore and weave together the different elements of whatever it is you are undertaking.

The decisions that lead you to achievements on the scale of the season are ones that are taken at key intervals and based on deep reflection about your direction. They are not day to day decisions about what actions to take at 11 this morning. To use our academic and athletic examples again, the 400 metre runner can't wake up each morning and figure out what event they're going to be training for today. That boat long since sailed and there will be years in which they never question it. It will probably be months at least between sessions of reflection to ascertain whether or not their training is making them the best 400 metre runner they can be. Meanwhile they get up and trust the process. And a college student doesn't wake up and wonder whether they should go to maths or history lectures today.

It's ultimately the fact that someone is training to be a 400 metre runner or an early modern history expert which determines that today they will be training hill repeats, or going to a lecture on Mary Queen of Scots. But not because they make the connection between those things afresh every day.

It would be easy to be dismissive and say they do those things because "that's what athletes and academics do." And that's true. But it's true because of the relationship between these three different timeframes - the day, the season, and the generation.

What that relationship is, and how you can use it to create your own jacquard training system to live your Sustainable Life Goals, is what we will cover now.

Vehicle-Project-Task

It will probably be little surprise that the three headings in the title of this chapter - vehicles, projects, and tasks - correspond to the three time periods of generation, season, and day.

The principles behind creating these headings are very simple.

First, to work with and not against our natural motivation mechanisms, and the way they both drive us towards the actions that will more likely lead to the life we want and respond to feedback to enable us to continue to pursue those actions.

Second, to ensure that you don't have to ask yourself every day, "What should I do now?" and spend all your time evaluating the relative merits and likely successes of potential actions. It takes away both the trivial, "What should I do today?" questions and the more existential or strategic, "Which things are most likely to give me my best life?" and "Will doing x, y, or z keep me on track or lead me astray?" kind of question. These are both vital sets of questions. But the place for them isn't clogging up you your bandwidth every day. The vehicle, project, task framework gives them full, but also appropriately limited, recognition.

Third, this system works with the natural rhythm of the jacquard system. It allows you to switch direction and shift the emphasis between areas of your Sustainable Life Goals at just the right time to ensure overall progress, and enjoyment of that progress. Think of it as a really effective gear changing mechanism that makes the changes smoothly, swiftly, and silently to match the conditions of the road.

Vehicles

The vehicle corresponds to the generational time period. It's the degree course, the athletic career, the portfolio investment. It is, that is to say, an umbrella heading for something that will happen over a significant (5-10 probably works best) period of time that sees you move through various stages towards increased mastery.

The vehicle is not, it is important to note, a "long-term goal" in the sense of "goals" that we have
been trying to avoid in this book. It sits underneath the Sustainable Life Goal as a heading for organising your life and your ambitions. And it is something that you will not only benefit from accomplishing but benefit from actually doing. The things you do within any vehicle will be things you have already identified that you enjoy - to the extent that is possible (a doctorate might be a vehicle, for example, and it might involve traveling new places, challenging the limits of your understanding, the experience of sitting in libraries, the stimulation of communicating ideas).

A vehicle will also usually be something that contributes to many Sustainable Life Goals at once. That will keep your interest and motivation, and make the best use of the limited resources you have. It will also make it easier for you to cycle your focus within the timeframe of the whole vehicle.

Let me illustrate the kind of thing that I mean by vehicles with two examples I have chosen: starting my own business, Rogue Interrobang, and something I call From 50 to 60.

That's exactly what it sounds like. An attempt to spend a decade pushing at my physical and mental limits to find out what kind of performance a 60 year old human being might be able to deliver with the right training and focus. It has, as is fairly clear, a 10 year horizon. My plan for Rogue Interrobang extends for 5 years.

Let me talk through both of these at a high level, and explain how they link upwards to my Sustainable Life Goals, before I go on to talk about the projects within them that help me make the progress I've mapped out that I want.

The first thing to say is to repeat what I've said from the start. Neither of these things is, or contains, a goal in the traditional sense of a point in time at which I can say I've made it but will then be left bereft and wondering where to turn next.

Instead, each of these vehicles represents a way to crystallise, over a motivationally meaningful period of time, the Sustainable Life Goals I have. From 50 to 60 captures that sense of pushing at the edge of potential that is possibly the most valuable experiential element of my life. It does so along the axis of physical capability and intellectual stimulation, the two big Sustainable Life Goals it works with. But I set it up intending to find ways to incorporate as many other of those Sustainable Life Goals as I could, in particular communicating - talking about what I'm doing, how I'm learning and becoming an expert in the techniques I develop.

Rogue Interrobang emerged from the most unlikely confluence of circumstances. I have never really thought of myself as someone who would or indeed could run their own business. I've always loved running what I'd thought of as projects. I ran a troupe of touring performance poets and musicians called The New Libertines for several years. I ran publishing collectives eight cuts gallery press and 79 Rat Press. And in sport, if there was any kind of team activity involved I was only ever happy as the captain. I loved making waves and I hated people telling me what to do.

But when it came to making money out of that trait, I'd always written it off. That was for other people. In particular, it was for people who didn't have my combination of mental illness and neurodivergence. And within that it was for people who weren't likely to get ill for weeks or months. And whose ability to do paperwork on their best days didn't fall short of an absent-minded professor on their worst days. So I imagined I would simply spend the rest of my days earning less than I needed to keep a roof over our head at a day job I despised doing the only things people would pay me to do.

For well over a decade I had been an administrator at the University of Oxford where I spent 10 years as a student before a spectacular breakdown during my doctorate left my dreams of an academic life in tatters - and the debt that followed the breakdown and years of poor mental health left any chance of ever completing those studies equally in tatters. I had resigned myself to pushing bits of (real and virtual) paper for people who had the job I'd always dreamed of. And it was destroying me slowly from the inside.

At the same time, in the mid 2010s, I had rediscovered my love of mind sports, and in 2016 went back to the Mind Sports Olympiad, the global gathering of mentathletes I'd first attended when it launched in 1997, where I'd won the World Intelligence Championships in 2000, but which I hadn't been to since 2001. It was one of those coming home experiences. Suddenly, after years of being a fish out of water, I was surrounded by people who shared my passion for pushing their mental performance, for discovering new paths to send the mind down, for expanding, and playing with the brain's plasticity.

That year and the following year I won the Creative Thinking World Championships. This was a time when almost every self-improvement or business advice article you read told you that creativity was the most important skill you could have to succeed in the new world in which we found ourselves. Yet here I was, a double world champion in this most prized of skills, and no one wanted to know. Let alone pay me for being creative. So I was stuck in a day job I tolerated at best.

And then an email turned up in my inbox for me to circulate to my academics. It announced something called the Oxford Humanities Innovation Challenge. Run by the university's innovation department, it was an attempt to get academics and students in the Humanities to be a little more entrepreneurial.

As a university, Oxford has a lot of spinout companies. We do a lot of world-leading research, and quite a lot of it ends up making the university money. We have companies that do everything from working on self-driving cars to protein folding; new chemical processes to, of course most prominently in the last few years, making vaccines. But if you just look at those things, you'd be forgiven for thinking we don't actually do any research in the Humanities. Which we do. A huge amount. Equally groundbreaking. But while some of it makes its way onto people's television screens and into bookstores, none of it at that point was making its way into companies.

The Humanities Innovation Challenge was designed to solve that problem. And as a faculty administrator, I had been asked to spread the message to my academics. But this was one of those rare messages that for some reason got my attention enough to read it first. And to do what I often do when I see competitions that pique my interest - go through to the terms and conditions to see what reason they give this time for me not to be eligible, so I could feel a sense of righteous indignation along with my seething resentment (as a self-published writer for well over a decade, being ineligible for competitions is something I am very used to). But however hard I scanned, I could see nothing to stop me.

This happened at just the same point where my frustration with no one wanting to pay me for being creative had crystallised into the thought that if I really was creative, I should probably be able to figure out a way to get people to pay me for it. And this competition seemed to be the perfect opportunity to put that idea to the test.

It was. I spent the weekend holed up in my office with a pile of A3 sheets, stacks of post-it notes, and a set of Sharpies. And by Monday morning I had come up with the idea for Mycelium, the creative thinking card game that was, as I put it to show that it had some relevance to my research, "based on the techniques of mediaeval monks and modern neuroscience."

The rest is history. I won the competition, and part of my prize was support from the university's innovation team that eventually led both to a beautifully designed and professionally printed set of Mycelium decks, and the founding of Rogue Interrobang. And here I am writing this book, which Rogue Interrobang will publish to sit alongside everything else we do with the aim of making the world more curious and creative.

The point of that story is to show how many of my Sustainable Life Goals are tied together in my endeavors with the company. There are, of course, some infrastructure goals. I know that any kind of regular day job I'm likely to get is not going to provide what I need financially for the rest of the life I want to live. Equally important, I know that running a company like Rogue Interrobang not only provides me with the opportunity to achieve that degree of financial freedom and security by providing an income through scalable as well as unscalable means, and possibly licensing. I know it also does so in a way that gives me autonomy of time within some parameters and a certain degree of geographical flexibility. And those mean that my ADHD is less likely to be an inhibitor to success than it is in a regular day job.

But the business feeds other Sustainable Life Goals. Its focus is on creativity and curiosity. Which could be the motto for my life. And the level of research I need to and am able to do to help further that provides the intellectual stimulation I need.

This is also the kind of business that requires me to communicate in exactly the ways I need to in order to lead my most fulfilling life. On the one hand, I get to write, to craft stories and share adventures in which I get to position my readers, you, as heroes on a journey. But, and this is why just writing or just focusing on the scaleable side of the business is never going to work. I also get to give talks and presentations, crafting a living performance on stage, getting the immediate feedback of watching an audience as I take them on a journey. And I get to run workshops, which allows me to communicate on a one to one level, to teach and adapt my stories to the individual needs of my audience.

Both of these vehicles are long-term enterprises that involve a number of Sustainable Life Goals. And while each has an end point, each also either leads seamlessly into another vehicle (60 to 70!) or will give way to another project (if I sell Rogue Interrobang, it will be because it has reached the value where such a sale means I can move to the phase of life where I can pursue the things that much money would enable me to pursue). And most important, there is not just one of them. I would recommend having a minimum of two vehicles at any one point. That way you will never reach the "what now?" point, even if one of your vehicles ends without an obvious replacement.

A vehicle in itself, however, isn't a particularly useful thing. It won't help you figure out what to do on a daily basis. Which is why the purpose of vehicles is, as the name suggests, to be filled.

Projects

A project is the name I use for a block of activity with a particular focus, that last in the spirit of the "season", around 3 months. Projects are literally the building blocks of vehicles. They are the term papers in a university degree; the training blocks in an athletic career; the product development in a business cycle.

Finding the right projects

Key to the success of your Sustainable Life Goals will be finding the right vehicles, and then finding the right projects to fill those vehicles.

As we saw when we looked at the season as a period of time, the project stands in relation to the vehicle as a term paper to a degree, or a training block to a sporting career. In order to fit within a vehicle, a project needs certain qualities.

These align with the jacquard principle we outlined above. Think of a project as what happens when you bring a particular thread to the fore in your life for a limited period of time. A well-defined project is the way of doing precisely that. The qualities it needs in order to achieve that are as follows.

First, a defined start and end point. This is what makes a project somewhat like a traditional "goal." What makes it different is that the end point of a project will not have a "what next?" factor. Because you will have another project lined up and ready to go. Remember that a project uses the motivational properties of the seasonal period to ensure that you move on just at the time you would naturally be looking for something else. It should "run its course." Which means that the end point of a project needs to stand in a realistic relationship to the starting point. For me that's a book of 25,000 to 35,000 words. It's a period of progressive strength training or distance training. It's a clearly-defined subject to learn.

Taking strength training as an example will illustrate how setting the end point of a project should fit the time period allocated. If my physical training is in a "strength" phase, I don't set myself a concrete goal. I won't look at my bench press, for example, and say, "OK, I can currently bench 70 kilos at 70 kilos bodyweight. I will train so that I can add 10% and lift 77 at 70 kilos bodyweight." Because that doesn't define an end point in time. I will say instead, for 12 weeks I will train with progressive overload, adding a little more weight or a little more volume each week. And I'll see where that gets me.

Second, it needs the right timing. By this I mean that projects should start at a point where you are ready and motivated to tackle them, and they should end before you get tired of them. The latter will usually depend on the first point we made above - ensuring that you have a clearly defined end point for the project.

The former, starting at a point when you are ready to devote three months to a project is something you can try to manage in several ways. The first again comes back to point one. Making sure you define a project with an end point that you can achieve in three months means you will work with your natural motivational cycle. That is, the "season" period is just the right length that your imagination is able to grasp, at the start of the period, the fact that through a certain course of action you will be able, all things being equal, to achieve a significant result. The time is short enough that you can maintain in your head the direct link between you of now and you of then, and there are few enough variables and uncertainties over a three month period that your imagination will be able to accept that much of the journey is within your control - too much longer and the probability of random events getting in the way starts to sky rocket. But the time is long enough that you can imagine significant progress.

The other thing you can do to ensure that you start projects at the right time is to keep a list of potential projects. This means you don't need to think what to do next while staring at a blank page or an empty journal.

My ADHD also means I have always had a lot of ideas come at me constantly for things that would make a great project. In the past, I have tended to dive into each of them the moment the idea came to me. Often that would be accompanied by an irresistible urge to kit myself out with new equipment, always with new notebooks, and inevitably with a new hyperfocused mindset. The result is one that will be familiar probably not just to other ADHD folk (though certainly to them). A history scattered with enthusiastically started but unfinished projects. And debt.

Keeping what is, in essence, little more than an "ideas file" has helped me to break this cycle. I will caveat that, as always, by saying I realise this might not work for other ADHD people, but it might be worth a try (and the method I outline below is one designed to work with the ADHD brain) - and for others, it's an invaluable tool.

You should keep your ideas box in the format that works best for you, be that digital or analogue (or possibly a combination, though I personally find it important to have everything in a single place).

I use a section of a physical journal, simply because I use that for everything. And I carry it everywhere with me so I can write things down as soon as I think of them and not have to worry either about them getting lost between one piece of paper and another or languishing in the voice notes on a phone. Other people use a box, whether that's something that can easily be organised like a card index box, or something more organic like a shoe box. And of course many people use software like Evernote or Notion.

If I get an idea for a project I will be sure to write down enough information to ensure that I can follow up later. But not so much that I start to get swept into a wave of excitement that could end up distracting me from the projects I'm already in the middle of. For me the latter part of that has always been harder than the former, and I have to write my notes mindfully, almost as though I am observing them from the outside, recording them for a future me who remains aware of what's needed yet detached in the present.

First, I will note down the idea itself - "create an online course about the history of mind palaces", for example. Then I will write down what the end of the project will look like ("online course materials live on Udemy"). I'll list the resources I think I'll need, and make a special note of any I don't have right now, along with some notes on how I think I might get hold of them. Again, for me this is a potential trigger point. My brain can get into a loop that it refuses to close, ruminating over missing equipment, nagging at me that the only way to move on is to go out and spend money I don't have - on something that right now is simply an idea. Too often in the past I've got into financial trouble by listening to that voice as the only way to quiet my brain. And then, because my overall approach wasn't under control, the money would of course be wasted because next week's project would take over almost as soon as I was started on that one.

And finally, I will list the Sustainable Life Goals I think the project will involve. I tend use a colour coding system for ease of reference, using coloured pens to make marks on the edge of the page corresponding to any Sustainable Life Goals involved, so that I can use them as an index even when the journal's pages are closed. This helps me to see at a glance what might be possible when it might be the right time to start

Third, the most important thing of all for a project. It needs to contribute to your Sustainable Life Goals. Whereas a vehicle will encompass many of your Sustainable Life Goals, the project will tend to focus on one. Which isn't to say that it will just involve one. Rather, following the jacquard principle, while several are there in the background, one will come to the fore.

The most obvious example of how this would work is a physical training block. If I want to concentrate, as an athlete, on building strength, I won't stop my speed or endurance training altogether. I will simply shift the balance and the intensity of my sessions.

Our example of the academic term paper demonstrates a slightly different element of the jacquard principle. I may be studying, say, 17th century Central European diplomacy (which, it happens, is something I am doing right now). That will feed my intellectual stimulation, sharpen my brain. But I might also give talks, go to common interest groups and meet people, and I might even take notes in a particular way that uses my creativity skills. The fact that I am involving all those other Sustainable Life Goals makes it easier for me to stay engaged, and benefits my progress in life overall.

Fourth, as well as fitting your Sustainable Life Goals, the projects you undertake at any time should fit within your vehicles. That's the way to ensure what feels like progress with the focus dialled in doesn't turn out to be moving quickly in the wrong direction when you then zoom out. If you are studying for a history degree, then spending a term learning topology won't take you very far in that direction. It's at this point that, when you look through a list of projects that excite you and they seem utterly disparate, you might want to go back and revisit your vehicles and ask if they need to be tweaked to allow you a much broader shift between projects.

Finally, projects should avoid, or mitigate, the blockers to acting that you identified earlier. There's no point having a project to learn skydiving if you're afraid of heights. It might well be something that brings you the adventure you crave - but if you're never going to get in a plane, or jump out of one if you do, then it's not a good use of your time to seek adventure in this way. At least not without first looking to overcome your fear.

Following those principles, you can evaluate your ideas. And you will soon build up a bank of potential projects from which you can choose when you need a new one. Which just leaves the question of how many projects to have on the go at any one time. The number that works for me is two to four. That's because for me that will cover all the bases of my Sustainable Life Goals.

And it's important that the primary focus of each project is different in order to weave together the best pattern, and to keep making overall progress in living the life you want. There is much to be said for the old adage of, at any one time, doing one thing for the mind, one for the body, and one for the soul.

Once you have decided on your projects, which fit perfectly into the motivational timeframe of the "season," the thing that remains is to have a way of determining what that means you actually do on a day to day basis.

Tasks

If the vehicle is what equates to the period of a generation, and the project what equates to the season, then what equates to the final key time period, the day, is "tasks." These are the actual things that need doing. The atoms that make up the object, as it were.

This all sounds very much less than radical. Is everything simply going to boil down to keeping a to-do list?

Kind of.

But only kind of. First, the thing about the tasks on your to-do list is that they will all fit within the projects you have already outlined. Just like your projects fit within vehicles and those vehicles are designed with your Sustainable Life Goals in mind. Any to-do list of tasks that you end up working from will be built specifically to stop you running fast and smoothly in the wrong direction (the problem when you launch into a new project every other week). Or more likely, just contribute nothing meaningful, which tends to happen when you do the same things you've always done for no reason other than that you've always done them.

To-do lists into which you put any kind of conscious effort are a surprisingly powerful corrective against "habits of a lifetime." Forcing yourself to write down all those things that serve no purpose but take time and resources (I'm going to go out on an unpopular limb here and use the example of ironing and folding the shirts you put on for casual wear - for me, I'd include the shirts you wear to work, but I know there are some concepts people need introducing to gradually, and maybe I really do work in a radically different environment from anyone else [hint, I don't]) will make you at least question just how necessary they really are. Especially if you look at your schedule and see you have no time for something that really would contribute to the life you want to lead.

And second, regular to-do lists can fail because they don't account for something really important. Not all tasks are equal because not all time is equal. Let me explain this by saying first what I don't mean. I am not talking about "mojo," to use an incredibly unhelpful term that has provided both endless bewilderment ("How do I go out for a run if I haven't got any mojo?" - well, put your shoes on, open the door, and start putting one foot in front of the other like you would any other day) and endless excuses ("I couldn't run today because I lost my mojo" - sure, but did you clean your teeth and do the dishes and all the other things that don't need "mojo"?)

What I mean is this. At various points during the day, our brains have windows during which they are capable of clarity that they lack at other times. In those windows, some things - especially deep work - will be easier than they are at other times. And some of those things will be possible only in those windows. It's a phenomenon most of us will recognise. We might experience it by noticing that a fog has suddenly cleared in the middle of doing something, whether that's playing with a spreadsheet, reading a book, thinking about a sales pitch, coming up with an idea for a YouTube video, preparing recipes for the week ahead. We have moments where what had felt like wading through treacle suddenly feels like freewheeling.

We will also have experienced the opposite. What seem like hours of unbroken flow suddenly hitting a wall, and our thoughts, our pen, the elegant chef's knife suddenly grinding to a halt as we start to fumble around like a runner caught at dusk without a headlamp.

It's easy to think of these windows of clarity as things we can learn to summon at will. And then to seek to find ways to do that. But while there are certainly things we can do to sharpen our minds and maybe increase the prevalence and duration of these windows of clarity (practising the best sleep hygiene we can, eating the right amount of the right food, exercising, keeping our minds sharp), we will also end up realising that trying to do this is more like looking for the philosopher's stone. The only people who really gain from such pursuits are the ones selling the apparent secret sauce - for everyone else there's frustration.

It is much more important, again, to have a mindful and intentional approach to this. Devote time to observing when during the day these windows tend to occur. Make notes by all means of what else is happening when they do, in case there are common variables such as sleep or eating or environment that you might reproduce. But most of all note the time at which your most and least clear-headed and focused times occur. You will probably find that the former happen for a couple of hours a day, up to three or four in some cases. As always, be honest, and be the best observer of yourself that you can be. And once you have enough information to spot the patterns, use it dispassionately and wisely.

Those few hours each day are possibly your most precious resource. The most important thing you can do with them is to protect them, where possible, and keep them for the tasks where that degree of clarity is most needed and most useful.

Of course, we live lives with commitments. And we don't live in our own little self-centred bubbles. We can't always tell the world to stop right now because it's our special time. So it's important to repeat one of the consistent messages of this book, which can be summed up in the phrase, "Don't let the perfect be the enemy of the good." Too much self-improvement sounds great on paper but is utterly unworkable in the context of real lives. And too much that seems to the author as though it might for everyone work will only actually work for them, because of the unique set of circumstances that, among other things, put them in the position where they had enough time in the day to write a book. And I don't care if you as an author think that by getting up at 4 in the morning everyone could write before the kids wake up and the boss starts getting antsy and emails start pinging and food needs prepping and runs need running. The fact you have a life and circumstances that makes getting up at 4 to write, actually having the lack of brain fog that means the page doesn't just swim in front of your eyes when you open it up, and being able to make it through the rest of the day intact - all that puts you in a position many of your readers can't begin to relate to. With the result that readers who try to put those things into practice will wonder why they are flogging themselves to burnout and seeing no results.

That's the reality check done. Consider it a given for everything in this book. And always remember that a programme of self-improvement that is going to last a lifetime has to work in your life. But that, of course, goes with another thing I have advocated throughout this book. Brutal honesty. Take stock of what your life will and won't permit. Unless that reflection is really frank and transparent and based on total honesty with yourself, you won't truly be in a position to know where your boundaries are. Boundaries and limitations are things that affect all of us. Where our own really lie is, however, something many of us aren't really realistic about because few of us are genuinely that honest in our assessment of our lives - and few of us reassess with the same honesty at regular intervals.

But there are some things we can control. Sometimes we have two things to do and two times in which we could do them. I might need to go for a run and write a key part of a talk. And I might have an hour free at six in the morning and an hour free at six in the evening. There's a lot of conventional wisdom and motivational posturing about the importance of running in the morning, and if I let that guide me I would head out for my morning run. I'd feel really great, and come back feeling really pleased with myself. Then by late afternoon, the realisation would creep up on me that I had left the clearest part of the day long behind me.

For much of my life, that's exactly the kind of decision I made. And inevitably I would come unstuck because my brain didn't work like the brain of whoever's advice I had just been reading. If I had paid primary attention to my own rhythms, the I would have realised that - if I could manage to be awake for it - there is almost always a window between about 6 and 7.30 that has almost magical properties. The fog clears, gears speed up, ideas that had bounced aimlessly begin to settle and have structure. My absolute priority is to capture those moments and use them for the things I can do at no other time. Whereas a run I can do with my brain in snooze mode.

And that brings me to the final point about tasks.

Resource-specific task lists

Build a list of tasks, based on your projects, that you break down according to what state you need to be in to undertake them. Let me explain what I mean.

Running and writing are very basic examples - and very personal ones - of the principle that different tasks can be performed with very different existing energy levels.

For me, there are four categories of task, corresponding to the different levels of clarity or energy needed to undertake them. It's likely to be different for you. But the principle will be the same. It's also likely that you will have two separate lists - one for the brain and one for the rest of the body. To go back to running, I can go out and jog a few miles in almost any state. If I need to do interval training with several high speed sprints, that's something I need to avoid doing if I'm pre-exhausted.

I'm not going to give too detailed advice on breaking physical things down into this kind of task category. That's because there are other factors involved around safety and avoiding injury. What I will say is that you should do it. And you can build a training plan you're much more likely to stick to if you have the flexibility that doing so affords you. If you need to do something on a Sunday, for example, but your body is screaming no to a long run, then it's very easy to shrug and give up. But if you have a list of short, non-exhausting things you can do even when your body's in what I would technically call "a right old state", then you can substitute in, say, some stretching. And occasionally a few minutes of stretching will warm you up enough that you could contemplate a set of curls or even lunges or air squats.

Stretching or air squats might seem like a poor substitute for a 10 mile run. But that misses the point. We're talking about the real world and those days when the choice isn't air squats or 10 miles but air squats or nothing. And we're talking about a whole lifetime over which that difference compounds. And on those days, having a list of alternatives that require the energy you do have rather than the energy you wish you had can make all the difference. And of course there may be other days when having that list means you can swap something that needs more energy because that's what you have.

So how are task lists structured? First, they need to be super specific. "Do some writing" isn't the kind of thing that's really helpful. Because the tasks on your list should all be things that you know will contribute to specific projects that you have. So you're looking for the level of detail that says, for example, "write 300 words of the talk for November's conference" or "read 10 pages of the textbook on early modern history." The point of being this specific is that you want to avoid running fast in the wrong direction. If you find yourself with free time just as your brain clears, you want to have ways of using it that you know will contribute to your Sustainable Life Goals.

Second, you need to figure out how to match tasks to the different energy levels you have through the day, week, or month. And that comes back, again, to honest self-observation. If you mismatch, then you will find yourself frustrated at what you can't do or underachieving compared to what you could do. Of course, you will get this wrong. Probably a lot.

So this breaking down of tasks by energy needs to be an iterative process. One of the things I learned very early on, for example, is that not all writing is the same. Writing a talk takes a lot more clarity than writing a book, for example. And that's largely because there's such a tight constraint on time.

What I realised over the course of time is that the part that takes the most clarity is forming the structure of something really concise, like a talk or a video where I've been given 2 or 3 minutes to make a point. The paragraph by paragraph breakdown of the few words I'm afforded is agonising. It involves decision after decision about what is truly essential, and the things I think I can't do without that are really just window dressing or distractions.

Once the structure is there, the actual writing is much more straightforward. The decisions have been made and the rest is much more like following a simple process. I can write chunks in time when I couldn't do any structuring. And the final part of the process, editing, is somewhere in between. The reason writing a book feels like it takes less really clear-headed time is because as a proportion of time spent, more of it is spent on the actual writing, and then the editing, and less on the structuring, than with a talk. And even the structuring is a little more forgiving because of the lower constraint level on word count.

So even within something that's only a part of what I do - my writing - I will be able to break down many tasks that all contribute to projects I'm working on. And I will be specific. "300 words of the book on accessibility," (level 2) "high level outline of a 2 minute talk on creative communication," (level 4) "editing 2000 words of the book on creative innovation," (level 3) "formatting a worksheet for my narrative analysis workshop" (level 1).

By breaking things down that specifically, I take the difficult "what do I do now?" questions out of the equation. And I provide myself a ready made checklist to ensure that every task contributes something to one of my current projects.

And the final part of the puzzle is to keep this list where it is always with you and you can flip straight into it when you want to know what to do. That will be whatever thing works for you. For me, it's in my paper-based journaling system, marked with a tab I can go straight to and laid out on a single page.

Other people will use note-taking or project management software. The important thing is that you use something that takes you as close to zero friction as possible to access. And ideally that you can use to create a checklist of what you actually did at the end of each day or at least relatively regular intervals.

Which brings me to my final point of the section. Monitoring and evaluating how you are doing in terms of the tasks you undertake each day. Again, this is something I do in my paper-based journal, but whatever software works for you is also good.

I find it really helpful to have a visual at-a-glance guide not just to the tasks I could do when I have the resources but the actual tasks I'm doing each day. And I try to do this across two axes where I can. First is the resource level of the task. And second is the area of Sustainable Life Goal the tasks are contributing to. This pattern that results from this should look fairly balanced. Ideally over the course of a month (the planner format I use to track this) i should be seeing a pattern that has some of every level of task, corresponding to the energy levels I'd expect during the month.

And I'd expect to see tasks fall across a wide range of Sustainable Life Goals, but be skewed slightly towards what I'm particularly focusing on according to the jacquard principle. To record this I use a simple colour code, with a different colour for each of my Sustainable Life Goals, in which I draw bars each day where the height corresponds to the time I spent on that task. This gives me an instant way of seeing, as regularly as week by week, if there are areas that I know I should be focusing on, and I know I have tasks for, but which I'm just not tackling. And then I can figure out what to do to fix that.

Principles for Acting

Everything we have said until this point is incredibly valuable. And it has been designed, unlike many self-improvement systems, around the fact that humans are anything but uniform and life is anything but straightforward. But even for all that realism, life throws us curve balls.

Some of those curve balls will be so dramatic, and will move unexpected things right to the top of the urgent pile, leaving no time for planning or preparation, at least not within the scope of this book, that will enable us to fit our response into a regular framework of Sustainable Life Goals. The mindful and intentional approaches outlined above are the closest we might get. They have certainly helped me deal with everything from death to financial emergency without the catastrophic levels of ongoing turmoil and trauma that marked my earlier decades. And of course regular consistent systems enable some things to tick over even during an emergency.

But this chapter is about a different level of unexpectedness. It's about how to make the kind of decision we face on a relatively regular level. The kind of decision that can often take us a lot of time to weigh up precisely because, unlike absolute emergencies, the answer isn't obvious. And the kind of decision that, cumulatively and over time, can cause considerable derailment of our lives if not tackled in the right way.

It is about the level of choice involved in deciding whether to go to a writing workshop or a concert that are running the same weekend. Whether to go for coffee with Sandra or cake with Samir on our day off work. And whether to say yes or no when an email pings our inbox with what seems like an interesting opportunity.

For me, ADHD has made this the most essential part of my toolkit. I have spent a lot of my life saying yes to every opportunity that came along and heading down every single rabbit hole I stumbled across. The result has been a breadth of experience that I probably couldn't have achieved any other way. But also a lack of real depth. To put it in the terms we've been using through this book, I've been great at pursuing projects but much less so at vehicles. Because when you're interested in everything, it's very hard to sustain focus on any one thing. Yet many Sustainable Life Goals, especially physical and financial ones, require lifelong focus.

To put it slightly differently, this is the difference between picking something up and becoming competent at it and developing a mastery. To use the oft-parroted and wrong but not really wrong figures, the former takes around 20 hours of focused deep work, the latter 10,000.

To solve this problem, we need to develop principles for acting.

These principles are rules of thumb. Tools for helping us to decide, when faced with something that might seem like an opportunity, or a choice that falls outside of the tasks we have on our list, what rabbit holes are worth a peep inside and which ones we should pass on by.

As I've done before, I'll outline the principles I've developed for myself, and explain very briefly the rationale behind each. Your will of course be different. But the categories covered, the way they are formed, and how they are used on a daily basis will help you to formulate your own rules of thumb so that the opportunities that present themselves enrich you rather than derailing you. So that you don't miss out on something you hadn't anticipated. But neither do you miss out on something you had planned because something else shiny has come along.

Some of these are specifically about choices. And some are about how to "be", moment by moment or more generally. In that sense they are an assistance towards being more mindful or more present or more intentional. Principles for mindset, that is, just as much as principles for action, are there to avoid drifting unawares into situations or futures by default rather than by choice.

What I have noticed in writing these out is how personal they are. They are correctives to faults I know I have. For that reason they will create a picture in any reader's head of the kind of person I must be. Probably not a very nice one. Which is an interesting thought in itself. And shows why I need such a list - because my deeply ingrained association of assertiveness with something morally questionable has caused so many opportunities to slip away over the years.

But more than that it shows how important it is to create principles that will take you from where you are to where you want to be rather than following a list.

Prioritise thorough rest

For me this is the most important principle for infrastructure. Many people train or do deep work too little. I know I do too much. At a high level I have the burnouts to show it. And when it comes to physical training, I spent the first four decades of my life starting endless exercise regimes by going all-in (by which I mean six long sessions a week, pushing to the absolute limit in each) and then ending up injured within a few weeks. I've now been training for almost three years at the time of writing without injury, making slow but consistent progress. I've built back up to around eight sessions a week, but that brings me to...

Do as much as possible in the green zone

You can't push to the limit in every single thing you do. If you try, you will make fabulous progress. For a few weeks. And end up back where you started. Continuous progress over long periods of time brings the most consistent rewards, especially if we are talking about the sustainable and lifelong bits of Sustainable Life Goals. And that means making choices every single workout to keep something in the tank.

"Today I will do what others won't so tomorrow I can do what others can't"

This comes from the American Football player Jerry Rice. I first came across it watching a documentary of Crossfit legend Mat Fraser. In that context it seems a strange principle to have sitting alongside two that are all about taking it easy. But rest and longevity are far from being about taking it easy. They are about playing it smart. They are the infrastructure principles that mean I can keep turning up to whatever I need to do every day. This is about reminding myself when I feel like garbage that feeling like garbage is no reason not to do a training or practice session (as opposed to feeling burned out or injured - again having the self-critical awareness and attentiveness to differentiate is key).

Remember I am the smartest in the room

This is something that sounds absurdly arrogant, but I wanted to be honest about what's on my list. Because if there's one thing I am trying to get across it's the importance of honesty when framing everything to yourself. And without showing how I do that, I can't expect anyone else to do likewise.

But let me also add some context. One of the things that has shaped four decades and more of my life has been my poor mental health, and - as I discovered in my mid 40s - being neurodivergent. One particular massive burnout as a result of a breakdown in my 20s led to me not finishing my doctorate and landing up with so much debt that I was never able to go back to it. That came after a childhood and early student career in which I was told the world was my oyster. It was taken for granted I would be an academic. And it fitted really well with what I wanted, as well as what I was good at. Especially if I could be the kind of academic like Carl Sagan who fell more into the "public intellectual" mould. Because I knew that as well as studying I loved to communicate what I'd discovered through that study.

The immediate aftermath of the breakdown was that the only job I could get, and the only way of paying even a portion of my bills while I could still persuade the banks not to call in the loans I'd taken out to do postgraduate study (not student loans that would have been income-dependent), was two days a week as a warehouse hand. Interestingly, it's a job I still look back on really fondly and probably marked the beginning of discovering that I not only enjoyed but was really quite good at physical exercise.

From there I eventually made my way back to Oxford, where I'd spent a decade studying, to become an administrator. With a broken CV, too much debt to repair it, and ongoing support needs for my poor mental health and worsening burnout from unrecognised ADHD it was the only job I could get that would pay me enough to keep a very basic roof over my head. I was shuffling papers, ironically doing the thing I am least competent at, for people who had the job I had not only wanted all my life but been told I would have if I just worked hard. Many of the people who had spent years telling me the value of my ideas now told me not to dare have an idea.

That's part of the background for needing to remind myself that the things that had made me really good at what I did hadn't gone away. That the pieces of paper and letters before and after someone's name aren't the things that make their ideas worth listening to.

Remember I can learn something from everyone

This is the flip side. It's what the people who treated me like I had lost every idea in my head once I returned to Oxford on the wrong side of the tracks had forgotten. Great ideas can come from anywhere. And things that could transform your life in particular can come from anyone. It's important not to chase mirages, and not to spend your whole life reading books that say the same as all the ones you've already read. But I've ended up finding one page that's transformed my life in the middle of a seemingly pedestrian text enough times to know that it's important to give things a hearing.

Living in Longhand

Don't do stuff for free

This again sounds really mean. But it embodies a realisation that there are only so many hours in a day. As a disabled person, I have fewer productive hours available to me than many others. And as someone who has been very publicly involved in many fields, in particular the writing world, I get a lot of people asking me to do stuff for free.

I have made two mistakes in the past. The first is desperately trying to people please. Not wanting to say no to anyone because that would make me a bad person. And certainly not to friends. At one point, when I was trying to break onto the performance poetry scene, I was spending so much time promoting and finding ways to support other poets that I had no time left at all to work on my own things. And when we all got on stage together it was evident I was rapidly becoming the weak link - because I was the one who had no time to work on their poetry. I ended up really resenting people who were friends I should have been delighted for. And I also ended up totally burned out on other occasions. I was frequently unable to follow through on the things I'd only said I'd do for fear of letting people down - only then to let them down. At which point of course many people forget that you only said yes as a favour because they'd put you in a tight spot. Saying no to "mates rates" is about protecting boundaries. And friendships.

On a more business level, I've noticed one thing is almost unfailingly true. The places that end up paying me to do things are almost always the places that paid me the first time. Gigs that start out with an offer of what free work might lead to inevitably lead nowhere but more free gigs.

Say "no"

And that leads to saying no more often. I've spoken already about the reasons I say yes too much - people pleasing and FOMO. The best way to stop saying yes is to learn to say no. Make it a go-to word in your vocabulary.

Make it easy for people to give me what I need

This is a tough one again because it goes against the people pleasing part of me. Which is why I need to make it a principle. This is especially the case in business. Naturally, I am very bad at what people would call a "funnel." I am also very bad at promoting myself or my products. This week I met a writer friend in the street and she asked me, "Can I buy Mycelium from the games shop in Oxford?" "No," I had to admit, because I felt awkward going in there and asking if they'd stock it. "Imagine they're someone else's," she said, adding, "I bet I could sell them for you." "And I bet I could sell your book to Waterstones," I concluded, pointing at the bookshop behind us.

So I don't think it's uniquely a me thing to find it easier to promote someone else rather than myself. And if that's you, then first you need to make it a habit to learn. But you also need to make it really easy. So now whenever I do a workshop, I always carry a pile of cards and books and put them on the desk so people can see them, and I have a slide at the end reminding people they're there along with a QR code to my mailing list. So even if I'm feeling really shy that day, it's still there.

Be careful with cash

This is a personal one for me. It goes back to some of the difficulties I had as a student when as soon as I'd taken £10 out of the bank, I'd mentally count it as gone. And then as soon as I looked in my wallet or emptied my pockets I'd find it was gone. As though it had leaked away without me noticing. I'd be in a shop and anything under £10, out came the note. And then the coins. And repeat. And contactless debit cards have made it so much worse.

Eliminating friction is one of my missions in life. As a result people are often surprised that I don't regard friction in all circumstances as a negative. But I do find it too easy to forget that behind the tap of the card or handover of coins there's a real figure that impacts my ability to keep a roof over my head. That means I need to create reminders and systems for myself to avoid simply frittering away any available balance. This needs to be a principle I act out daily as well as a key part of the financial aspect of my Sustainable Life Goals.

Look after things

I'm dyspraxic. And one of the things that means is that I break things. Not deliberately. And not through carelessness. My lack of coordination in some situations means that there are areas on my desk, for example, where if I leave something it WILL get knocked off.

So looking after things is more than just a matter of not wasting money by wearing things out or damaging them by neglect. It's an issue of constant vigilance. If I so much as see something in one of those areas on my desk I will move it as soon as I catch sight. Likewise, I think before I put things down or pick them up.

And, of course, generally looking after things comes as well.

Read

It's amazing how easy it is to forget to do even the things we love doing when life gets ridiculously busy. And reading is one of those things. I always have more than one book on the go, which is one strategy to make sure I can always dip into something that appeals. And I both take a book with me everywhere I go and leave books lying around so if I have a spare moment there's always one there I can turn to.

Journal more efficiently

Journaling is a very personal subject for me. My ADHD means I have spent years trying to find a way of journaling that actually works. And by works, I mean, "combines the different functions I need it to perform." Journaling with ADHD is a minefield and a fine art in one.

Those functions form a pyramid. At the base of the pyramid is, "Not missing appointments." Which sounds really basic, but I have spent my whole life missing I would say around a quarter of even the most urgent appointments. ADHD plays some real gems of tricks on your brain and one of those is "object impermanence." This means that if something is not right there in front of you in plain sight, your brain treats it as though it doesn't exist. Sometimes this can be as extreme as writing down a note while you're talking to someone and if you don't hold that note in your hand then before they've finished speaking, its existence is gone. It also means only one screen on my computer ever stands a chance of being seen - but then only if I think to open it. And if I am looking at a computer screen, then a sheet of paper next to it might as well not exist. So if someone adds an appointment for me in Outlook, someone else in Google calendar, something else is a standing engagement, and someone else arranges something when we meet in person, the chances of those all getting remembered? Zero. And what really messes with people's heads is that at the same time I'm a competitive memory athlete.

All of which is to say that journaling is a cornerstone of managing to function in the world at all for me. So finding ways of doing it better is really important.

Tell stories that centre me in the fulfilment of people's dreams

This is at the heart of running a business like the one I do. Creativity, the way I teach it, is about unlocking people's potential. And the techniques I help people develop go way beyond the usual creative thinking tips. It's what I call "cradle to grave creativity." That is, I start with fostering the conditions in which new ideas are born. And I take those ideas right through to the point at which they're implemented.

For me to tell the story around that means I have to be able to do more than say "I teach creativity." And it has to be less cheesy that, "I help you make your dreams come true."

Develop compelling products and make them the best they can possibly be

One of the sayings I need to hear more than any other on a regular basis, which isn't on this list, is, "Don't let the perfect be the enemy of the good." Perfectionism has got me into a lot of trouble over the years. It's one reason so many things have remained undone in my life. And your list would probably benefit from it - alongside things like "just hand it in as it is" and "good enough is good enough" and "get the thing out there and tinker later." It's part of the ethos of "move fast and break things" and goes with the agile, lean, and iterative approach that has become very popular in the wake of the rise of Silicon Valley.

But I've recently also realised how important it can be to get the core parts of something the best they can be while you're still building in the shed. That's time you will never get back when the thing you're building is out there. You can't undo the first look someone gets at a thing. And in a crowded marketplace like self-improvement (and, indeed, games) that first look needs to make people's jaw drop.

Use tech better

I am far from a Luddite. I love technology. But my ADHD means I struggle with a lot of it. And that can leave me in an all or nothing situation. So when faced with situations where I need to use technology or am offered the opportunity to use technology, I have tried to develop a system of decision-making questions to allow me to make the most of the technology I need while not overloading my system with tech I won't use. This involves very strict management of passwords and multi factor authentication, and a full exploration of actual as opposed to supposed benefits. And most of all, finding out what I can about alternatives. Simply signing up or downloading an app for "simplicity" is something I've learned can actually cost me hours and hours over the long term.

Extract value from BS tasks

This is probably the most valuable and the most widely applicable principle of all. We all have to do things every single day simply because they are essential. For many of us this will include our day jobs. It certainly includes paying bills and household administration, from looking after finances to doing the dishes. Given that we have to do these things, the question becomes: how can we approach these tasks so that we learn transferable skills from them that we can then apply to the tasks that are truly valuable for the life we want?

This not only means that BS tasks can become useful. They can also become fun, as figuring out the way to extract value from them becomes a challenge that can lift our minds out of the mundanity of the task itself. I find it also helps me to approach these tasks more mindfully. I am able to avoid the frustration I felt for so long because I know deep down there is a purpose to what I do. And that in turn means I can focus more completely on those tasks and gain satisfaction and mastery of them. And I am less likely to leave them undone, avoiding all the problems that would entail.

Develop systems

Having standard operating procedures for tasks and choices takes away the need for deliberation. This can work for anything from your morning routine to how you set up a journal. Just make sure that they have enough flex to cope with the unexpected. Otherwise you can end up never going away anywhere you really want to in case it messes with your morning routine, for example. Remember that your systems are there to free you up to do what you want to do rather than the life you lead being set up so you can follow your systems.

Schedule things in advance

This is less about filling my diary and taking away the flexibility to say yes to exciting opportunities than it is about making decisions early if I know they have to be made. It's also about scanning the horizon (or journal) for distant elephants and trying to schedule work to tackle them before they begin to loom.

Do paperwork in advance

My ADHD means paperwork usually gets done right at the last minute because of the complex relationship between deadlines and adrenaline. But the adrenaline kick a deadline gives activates the circuits that use my clearest, most valuable time in the day. So I try to avoid wasting that precious resource on paperwork if I possibly can. That means I'll try to block out an time for it, while accepting that sometimes it just won't happen.

Take credit when it's mine

Another one that's explained by lots of the things I've said before. If I do something, the easiest thing when someone says something nice about it is either to dismiss it with, "It's nothing," or to pass all the credit elsewhere: "It was only possible because of..." The problem is that other people, the ones you see rise up the ranks around you, don't do that. They'll take the credit you reflect at them and add it to the spotlight they already shine on themselves.

Be memorable

This is something I've tended not to struggle with. A combination of bipolar and sensory issues with clothes means I have rarely dressed like other people dress, and I know I don't behave like other people behave or do social interaction the way others do. That's half the battle. The other half is associating that difference in people's minds with something positive, specifically with creativity and value, so when they're looking for someone to turn to they think of me.

Use the power of compounding

Small steps over a long time. It gets harder to go all in on this as you get older. But even in my early 50s I have seen how benefits can compound over time. This has been especially noticeable with my health and fitness, both in getting to my ideal weight, and in training consistently over a long period rather than going into a training programme helter skelter and blowing up injured after a few weeks like I'd always done in the past.

It took me two and a half years to lose the seven stone I needed in order to get where I wanted to be. When people who saw me before and after ask me "what diet were you on?" or "what programme did you use?" (Something that happened a lot because I started the journey at the beginning of the pandemic so there were a lot of people who said goodbye to me when I was 19 stone and then didn't see me again until I was 12). They often don't like the answer, "one that I can stick to for the rest of my life."

In practice what I did was start by replacing one thing with something smaller. And I did that for a month. And then I replaced something with a high calorie density with something that had a lower calorie density. And did that for six months. And at the same time I added one session with a kettlebell each week. For a month. Then increased that to three easy sessions a week, for six months. Then one run a week, then two, never pushing myself out of the green zone. I never lost more than a pound a week. But I rarely lost less.

Francis of Assisi

We've talked about this a lot so it needs no further explanation. Knowing what you can and can't change and then pursuing or leaving be is a skill that saves so much time and disappointment. Recognising the importance of this, I have made the 13th century monk-turned-saint into a verb.

Ground myself. Compose myself. Breathe. Take up space.

This final one is about how I occupy time and space, in both a figurative and a literal sense. The first part is about what I would call bringing myself back to the present. I've talked a lot about mindfulness in the sense of being present in the moment, and being very intentional about the decisions you take and the actions you perform. But that isn't easy. And one of the things that helps me with it is having some simple actions I can perform that bring me back into that intentional and present state when I feel what I think I would technically call "scattered" or more colloquially call "all over the place."

It might sound like something straight from the thumbnail of a wellness influencer, but the main thing I do to help me recentre myself in time and space so that I can proceed with more deliberate intention is focus on my breathing. There are lots of people more expert than me on this, but the kind of breathing technique I use is "box breathing." This is a very regular form of breathing which involves breathing in, holding, breathing out, holding, and repeating - spending an equal amount of time on each of those four actions.

At the same time as I am box breathing, I will imagine pieces, like shards of a broken glass, coming together from every side of me and reforming, whole, in my body. Doing this for not even as long as a minute can dramatically refocus my thoughts and take me out of many states of helplessness or anxiety that arise from being unable to organise my thought process.

The second part of this is about how I occupy space physically. Again, this can sound a little bit like "straighten your spine" or "shoulders back, chest out, stomach in" or a ton of other things that have a spurious relationship to anything other than placebo. But it's part of the earlier "be memorable" principle.

Despite being a performer, and loving nothing more than being on stage in front of an audience, when I step off the stage I have always struggled with confidence, with knowing how to navigate the social space. The result is that I have tended to shrink, physically, into myself. It became almost a way of avoiding having to figure out how to interact. If I just became invisible, no one would notice me and the problem would go away.

The result is that I have spent most of my life being unable to get served at bars and cafes even when I want to be noticed, because people simply ignore me. They push in front of me in queues, blank me in meetings, act for all the world as if I really were invisible.

What this means is that while I might be able to disappear when I want to, the lack of "presence" has spilled over into other areas of my life where it's anything but advantageous. Most problematic of all has been the way shrinking into myself physically has been tied up with a lack of confidence. Unless I'm on the stage, which is somehow different, I spent most of my life in a mental place where I didn't take up space because I didn't believe I had a right to occupy space. "I'm not worth it" is somewhat of a cliché, but for many people it's at the heart of why they do or fail to do things that from the outside seem strange.

This particular principle, to be clear, isn't "be more confident." That's not something we can choose to do with a simple flick of a switch. But the effect of constantly reminding myself to adopt a posture that occupies space has a remarkably noticeable impact on my confidence as a by-product.

Your principles

Your principles will be different from mine. But the, er, principle behind them will be the same. They are the final piece in the toolkit of living out Sustainable Life Goals. Their purpose is to help you in situations where you:

Face the unexpected and have no frame of reference. The unexpected can be a source of opportunity or threat. But it is most commonly a source of confusion, anxiety, and uncertainty. The lack of a frame of reference for unexpected events means that the algorithms we use in daily life of the "if x happens, do y" variety break down. Which is why it's important also to have algorithms that help us in unexpected circumstances. But they have to be flexible enough to accommodate whatever those circumstances may be. A significant point of having principles like the ones outlined in this chapter is to minimise the anxiety of the unforeseen: and the time we spend figuring out what to do. Instead of saying, "I've not experienced anything like this before: help!" we can say, "I've not experiences anything like this before: but that's OK, let's break it down and figure it out."

Want the freedom to be spontaneous without undoing the progress you've made or setting yourself on an unhelpful track. This will include situations where a surprise opportunity comes your way or an invitation arrives out of the blue. You might have enough time and energy that, yes, you could do it, but that would mean not doing something else. If you say no to every opportunity simply because it doesn't fit an existing Sustainable Life Goal, you'll end up living a life on a very narrow set of rails. If you say yes to everything, you'll end up adrift and discontent and wondering why you never finish the things you start. For me, principles like doing nothing for free are key to making these decisions. Obviously they can be overridden, but only with a compelling case. My spouse has a really useful set of questions to apply as a filter in these cases. The two most important are, "Which level of my Maslow's pyramid most needs feeding right now?" and "Which levels of the pyramid would this feed?" (Maslow's pyramid is a way of arranging the different needs people have in ascending order of how essential they are for human survival and for achieving the next level - we have done something similar in this book by talking about infrastructure goals as well as those built on them). The final question is, "What resources (in all senses) will doing this cost me?" The equation one is trying to solve is, "Will this give me what I need right now without too great a cost for that benefit?" Because what we need will change as our situation changes. Sometimes, when we're in a place of comfort, fun and intellectual challenge is really valuable and worth spending resources on. At other times we need to divert all the energy we can to shoring up more fundamental needs like financial security or emotional connection with loved ones. At times like that, going and doing the fun-but-exhausting thing might have a catastrophic effect.

Don't have anything particular to do. A lot of the time, no matter how much preparation we've done and task lists we've got ready, we simply don't have any easy choices available to us. Maybe we have an unexpected wait in a place where we have no access to the things we would have used to do our tasks (our battery may have run down, or today the weather was bad so we didn't bring a book with us). What do we do at times like that? It can be good to have a principle to help, even if it's only a principle that tells us it's OK to chill! Being given permission to focus on deep breathing can be more restorative than sitting there fidgeting, feeling we should be getting on.

Know that you are in danger of being derailed. This is something we face on a daily basis. Whether we're trying to live a healthy lifestyle or trying to avoid letting days slip by while we scroll through social media, it is really easy to find ourselves in situations where we simply drift into doing things we wish we wouldn't. And the best way to avoid that is to identify the situations in which it happens most often, and to provide ourselves with default actions instead of the things we want to avoid. Or to take the even more pragmatic approach of avoiding some situations altogether. Principles for acting are a great way of doing that. They give you a "when in x situation, do y" option that short circuits the thing you want to avoid. It may be "when I'm in the kitchen, grab an apple," or it may be "when I sit down, pick up my book." Or it may be one level back, "Don't go to the kitchen in the afternoon." And to support those principles, you can take steps to create an environment in which they work well. Keep apples on the kitchen side. Keep a book by the sofa. Or keep a big jug of water with you so you have no reason to go to the kitchen.

Conclusion

This book is about helping you to reframe the way you view "goals" so that by pursuing the goals you set, you get out of life what you really want to. It gives you a very flexible template that will help you avoid the disappointment that comes with traditional goal setting, and means that you never arrive at your dreamed of destination only to get there and find yourself asking, "Is that it?"

Let's end with a chronological recap of the steps we outlined in your quest to set, and put in place a system to pursue and attain, your Sustainable Life Goals.

Imagine you are living your ideal life
↓
What things are fundamental to it? Keep questioning these, asking "Why do I want this?" until you reach the absolutely essential elements
↓
Frame these as 6-10 **Sustainable Life Goals**
↓
Identify the **infrastructure goals** among them (health, finance, home/shelter, relationships) that will help you live a life pursuing these things
↓
Identify whether you tend to look to **the past or the future**
↓
Identify whether the **barriers** you have faced so far in life have tended to be **external or internal hard or soft**
↓
Assess how your answers might help you ensure the things you have identified work for you
↓

Figure out your "**blockers**," things that stop you doing what would help you pursue your Sustainable Life Goals, and establish strategies to work with or around these

↓

Use the **jacquard model** to create in turn:

↓

Vehicles that over 5-10 years will enable progress towards all of your Sustainable Life Goals

↓

Projects of around 3 months to fill each vehicle that will enable you to make continual progress without ever getting bored

↓

Tasks, broken down according to the resources they take, that will successfully see these projects through, so that you don't have to make unnecessary choices on a daily basis

↓

Establish **principles for acting** that will help you to do these tasks, and to face uncertainty and opportunity in such a way that you use them to further the things you want from life

↓

And every 6 months, **revisit your Sustainable Life Goals** to see whether they are still right.

Epilogue

6 August 2023. Morning

The sun crept over the horizon many hours ago now, and the residue of yesterday's rain has already burned away. My legs tighten slightly as I pull the iron from the floor of the University of Oxford's trackside gym, but no more than slightly. The weight I'm deadlifting is little more than my 75kg bodyweight, but it is enough for now.

The track the old school metal and stone gym sits beside is the famous Iffley Road track. I watch the track as I lift. The last remaining warriors hobble and stumble the final few laps of the 24 hour race that owes its name, the Bannister Series, to the far fewer but considerably faster laps Sir Roger Bannister completed 69 years before.

Until 10pm last night, I had been one of them. After what had seemed like a dry early summer, all the rain that hadn't fallen felt like it had come at once. The floor of the tent where some of the runners had left their dry clothes and supplies had become a lake. The imperfect drainage of university running tracks had become very apparent. Attempting to keep feet dry was a Sisyphean task. In the first half of the 12 hours I was out there I got through 6 pairs of socks. At that point it was clear the only thing the attempt to seek out dry cloth was achieving was delay. My feet were already soaked and softening. Blisters were inevitable. Pain was inevitable. Missing my target of 50 miles in under 12 hours was not. Unless I kept stopping for a futile kit change.

After 11 hours and 47 minutes as I approached the start/finish line I called out to the timer, bracing against the conditions in a dry robe of which I had grown increasingly envious, "50 miles is 202 laps, is that right?" He gave me a nod. "And this is the 201st I'm finishing now?"

Another nod, and I broke into the broadest of smiles and the swiftest of canters (so much as macerated feet decorated with blood blisters are capable of swiftness or canters) and, after 201 laps of steady metronomic pace, I maintained both the smile and the speed for one final, furious effort.

As I crossed the line, reached down to my ankle and removed the timing chip that I handed back with a joyful, "that's me done, thank you so much!" I punched the air in delight, packed my kit bag, and headed back into town.

This smile didn't fade as I hefted my foot over the sink and splattered watery blood across the bowl. I was already looking forward to what came next. That particular stage in my journey got underway the next morning, as I returned to the track, loaded the barbell, and began to pull.

As I lifted, I watched the battered heroes one by one break out of a painful walk to beat the countdown for one last lap. I knew what every one of them would be doing the following day. Limping. Nursing themselves. I wondered how many of them would also be asking, "What now?"

Acknowledgements

Most of the ideas in this book germinated, took form, and became practically applicable during the endless long walks with my spouse that are an integral part of our ideal lives. Anything truly insightful or original is theirs. Anything incompletely articulated or insufficiently useful is mine.

This is the first book published by Rogue Interrobang Press. It has always been one of my ambitions to make Rogue Interrobang the O'Reilly Tools of Change of the creative mind and body. If I succeed, this will have been the first step, and one that was only possible thanks to those who have helped Rogue Interrobang reach this point. At Oxford University Innovation, Mark Mann, Chris Fellingham, Serena de Nahlik, Pippa Christodoulou, and Richard Auburn were and still are essential in encouraging me and enabling me to follow the dream.

A very special thank you to Andrew Fairweather-Tall, who championed what I was doing within the Humanities Division at the University of Oxford when it would have been so much easier not to. And above all, my deepest thanks to Vicky McGuinnes at TORCH, for providing me with so many wonderful opportunities to present what I was doing to the public. Without the mentorship and encouragement of Robert Hocking, Guy Gadney, the Jasons, Cath Spence, and all involved in Oxford's innovation ecosystem I would have dropped off the radar long since. A very particular thanks to Chris Fitch, who for two decades has been a co-conspirator and my guardian angel.

To everyone who has allowed themselves to be my guinea pigs, from the children of Cheney School to the marketing team at Malaberg, and especially so many dear friends and champions: your feedback and enthusiasm brings what I do to life.

For this book in particular, of course I owe a huge debt to all whose lives show that you do not have to follow a single path in life, and that happiness is a thing often found scattered on many trails. Many of them I read about in books or saw on screen, but my life has been deliciously larded by encountering them. Etan Ilfield, Veronika von Volkova, Aki Schilz, Nelson Dellis, Joanna Penn, Tom de Freston, and Jane Dixon Smith, to whom I owe an enormous dent also as my brilliant cover designer, have all been beacons to light my way. And of course no light has shone more brightly or in more colours than my spouse.

Milton Keynes UK
Ingram Content Group UK Ltd.
UKHW022253150124
436080UK00014B/1570